Renewal in Late Life through Pastoral Counseling

 *Integration Books*

Renewal in Late Life through Pastoral Counseling

James N. Lapsley

Integration Books

paulist press/new york/mahwah

For Helen

Copyright © 1992 by James N. Lapsley

Library of Congress Cataloging-in-Publication Data

Lapsley, James N.
   Renewal in late life through pastoral counseling/James N. Lapsley.
      p.   cm.—(Integration books)
   Includes bibliographical references.
   ISBN 0-8091-3333-4
   1. Aged—Pastoral counseling of.   2. Aged—Religious life.
3. Spiritual life—Christianity.   I. Title.   II. Series.
BV4580.L355   1992
259'.3—dc20   92-19818
                                                                  CIP

Published by Paulist Press
997 Macarthur Boulevard
Mahwah, New Jersey 07430

Printed and bound in the
United States of America

Contents

Acknowledgments

The encouragement of Robert J. Wicks, the General Editor of the Paulist Press series, Integration Books, to undertake this study of pastoral counseling in late life, is greatly appreciated, as is his unfailing support during the researching and writing of the book.

My gratitude goes to the Princeton Theological Seminary, its president, Thomas W. Gillespie, and its Board of Trustees for a year's sabbatical leave, during which most of the research and writing of this book was completed, and also for a research travel grant which provided for much of the expense of a sojourn in the retirement communities near Phoenix, Arizona, in the winter of 1990.

I owe a multiple debt to my wife, Helen Winter Lapsley, whose knowledge of and experience in a retirement community has been invaluable, and whose careful comments on the manuscript and personal support during the weeks of its preparation have been unfailing and always encouraging.

My thanks go to Faith Presbyterian Church of Sun City, Arizona, its senior minister, Francis W. Park III, its other ministers, its Session, staff, and members for their hospitality shown me during a two-months stay in January and February of 1990. I am grateful, too, to other professionals in the Phoenix area for their time and interest in this project—particularly to Duane Halloran, James W. Hagelganz, J. Davis Illingworth, Ray Gibson, and Robert V. Martz.

I appreciate the hospitality of the Suzanne Paterson Center, Princeton, NJ, and its director, Gilian Godfrey, during the fall of 1989, when I shared in some of their rich life together; also the hospitality and insights of Chaplain W. K. Childress of the Asbury Methodist Village, Gaithersburg, MD.

Finally, my thanks go to Dorothy Hullfish, my secretary, for the preparation of the final draft of the manuscript, and for conversation about families and aging over several years.

James N. Lapsley
Princeton, NJ
July, 1991

Foreword

In *Renewal in Late Life through Pastoral Counseling* James Lapsley offers us a positive theology and a practical psychology of aging in a succinct yet rich manner. Because of this, his work is of value to those who are involved in either informal or focal, sustained help for the elderly (i.e., persons in general ministry or pastoral counseling). It is also a helpful resource for concerned adult Christians who are looking for a practical treatment of this timely topic.

Professor Lapsley begins the volume by dispelling some of the primary myths about ageism. In this pursuit he shows that one of the main underlying sources of such inaccurate views of the elderly (even by many in professional ministry) is the attempt to superimpose a model of spiritual and psychological health used with young adults on persons in late adulthood.

To deal with this, he provides ideas and themes that form the basis of a broad theological anthropology which helps us understand the final season of life. He argues rightly for the importance of what he refers to as a "self-spirit" type model which allows us to view ministry to the elderly in a more wholistic fashion. Whether one agrees with all aspects or not with such a model, certainly it will provoke a train of thinking more open and respectful to the distinct needs, goals, and challenges of informal/formal ministry with elderly persons.

Following his theoretical remarks, the second half of the book provides a fine array of practical techniques and a welcomed glimpse into actual age-segregated contexts in which pastoral care/counseling of the elderly is done. His appreciation and illustration of certain basic essential age-related pastoral counseling techniques helps to bring to life how a helper can apply general object relations and cognitive theoretical ap-

1

proaches in a way that is most meaningful with this population. In this section we are guided in methods to assist older adults to take such steps as: reduce discomfort or conflict, enable better decision making, reframe/decatastrophize events, and to take clear steps toward further consolidation of the self when faced by past guilts and earlier rejections which often reemerge at this stage and lead to distress, depression, and anxiety.

Overall, the spiritual and psychological wisdom in this book made me realize more than ever that many of the anxieties and dilemmas of the elderly are not only sad but also in many cases *unnecessary*. James Lapsley in *Renewal in Late Life through Pastoral Counseling* has provided the church with a book that is both thought provoking and practical. He has helped me begin to increase my sensitivity and skills in an area that I had many misconceptions about without even realizing it. It is a book I can honestly say provides glimpses of understanding that indeed set the stage for *metanoia* in our necessary ministry to the elderly. In this primer on the pastoral counseling of the elderly, he has offered us his research, clinical acumen, and his own philosophy of the Christian life of the elderly in a clear and compassionate way so that we may walk with those in late adulthood in a more intelligent and spiritual way. And for this, I am truly grateful.

Robert J. Wicks
Series Editor

Chapter 1

Anxieties and Dilemmas of the Elderly

1. *Representative Vignettes.* Jean, a widow of 80, lives in her own home in a small city in the midwest. She has lived there for many years—alone since her husband died eight years ago. Her two sons live with their families in distant parts of the United States. She has been active in her community and attended church regularly until recently. She still drives her ten-year-old car, which has been taking increasing bites out of her modest fixed income. Her house seems to be constantly in need of repairs which she feels she can ill afford. Her health has been generally good for a person her age, but now arthritis has begun to take a toll on her physical capabilities and her morale.

She worries a lot now about the future. How long should she continue to live alone? Will she have to give up her car? Where might she go? She wonders if she is not facing the end of her life and her personhood. She does not dare let her sons know about these anxieties, lest they try to whisk her off to a nursing home, or perhaps even worse, try to get her to move in with one of them—for six months, and then to the other for six months. As she thinks about them, traumatic events that took place long ago, disturb her. She is beginning to slide toward depression.

Bill, in his late 70s, takes care of his wife, Sue, who has had a stroke, leaving her partially paralyzed. The physical and emotional tolls that this takes on him are compounded by chronic troubles they have had in their marriage for many years. Bill is considering placing Sue in a nursing home, or moving with her into a multilevel retirement center. He ponders the economic cost and at the same time worries about living with Sue in the small quarters of the retirement center, or, alternatively, about his probable sense of guilt for placing

3

her in a nursing home, where she says she does not wish to go. He has some help at home with Sue, but it does not seem to be enough, especially since he is left alone with her at night.

These two vignettes represent not unusual persons and circumstances among the elderly population, and their anxieties and dilemmas. Often their needs are not addressed, or else are inadequately addressed by pastoral caregivers and others who seek to assist the elderly. For the most part ministers and other caregivers tend to offer the elderly supportive pastoral care on an informal basis, which in many instances is adequate, but not pastoral counseling, which may well be needed in cases such as those cited above. Jean and Bill need some focal, sustained help in clarifying the issues facing them, both the internal cognitive and emotional issues, and the external reality issues.

For reasons that will be discussed in more detail later on in this book, both caregivers and the elderly tend to resist pastoral counseling. Suffice it to say here that many caregivers feel that the elderly are resistant to change, or at least very difficult to work with when deeply personal issues are in focus, and that many of the elderly feel that counseling and psychotherapy are threats to their independence, and even to their self-esteem and identity as persons.

Underlying this mutual resistance is a fundamental issue that pervades our society's view of the elderly and its attempts to relate to them. *The models of what a human being is that are used by professionals and lay people alike are of young adults.* These may be stretched into middle age, but they do not stretch to cover the elderly, who are consequently regarded as not quite human, or at best as second-class citizens. In western Christian theology Paul of Tarsus, Augustine of Hippo, young Martin Luther, and more recently, Thomas Merton, are the models. In the helping professions oriented to psychology, Freud and his followers provided the basic model, now supplemented by others organized around the notion of self-actualization (a phrase first made popular by C. G. Jung, who with his emphasis upon middle age, constitutes an exception to the young adult model—but an exception too arcane to have significantly influenced the basic paradigm). That all these models were in their original form those of young adult *males*—a situation only now beginning to be rectified by some feminist revisionists, such as Dinnerstein and Chodorow, further compounds the problem.[1]

Erik Erikson and pastoral theologians who have followed his lead, such as Browning and Capps, have mitigated this problem to some extent, but their normative starting point still seems to me to be the late adolescent or young adult.[2] Old age is a holding operation in which the best that can be done is to find and hold one's integrity, based on identity previously acquired, perhaps with a few embellishments.

A theological anthropology intended for all seasons of life will be presented in this book. Further, it is intended to be comprehensive of the full range of humankind viewed cross-sectionally, that is, to include both sexes in all cultures. However, it must be acknowledged that the starting point is western culture, beginning with works traditionally attributed to Moses and Homer. No pretense that it is a culture-free model is made. I believe that if the model is adequate for an understanding of the elderly, and for their full humanity, it will also be adequate for understanding those phases of life which led up to more advanced years.

2. *The Literature.* There is a growing literature about the pastoral care of the elderly, some of which touches on pastoral counseling (eg., William Clements' *Care and Counseling of the Aging*[3]). The bulk of the literature focuses upon pastoral care in a more general sense, with the emphasis upon more casual and mainly supportive pastoral care, in which each encounter is essentially discrete, even though there may be a certain amount of thematic continuity. This kind of pastoral care is, of course, of great importance in assisting the elderly, but it is my contention in this book that it is not always sufficient.

Some occasions and problems call for more extensive and/ or more focal helping, a particular form of pastoral care we call pastoral counseling, which is also characterized by a verbal "contract," or understanding about the focus of the counseling and about time and place of meeting. There is little in the literature about the specific goals of such pastoral counseling, or about its procedures. To these questions this book is specifically addressed, albeit with a lot of space devoted to theoretical and background materials which I think are necessary to understand it properly.

There is more literature about theoretical dimensions of the questions about aging within and adjoining the scope of pastoral and practical theology that is pertinent to this study. K. Brynolf Lyon's *Toward a Practical Theology of Aging*[4] presents a normative view of aging which has considerable pertinence for the present study. Earlier volumes edited by Seward Hiltner[5] and by Carol and Perry LeFevre[6] also contain materials that are relevant. Eugene Bianchi's *Aging As a Spiritual Journey*[7] is particularly valuable as an insightful focus upon the dimension of spirit, a key issue in this book.

3. *Needs and Situations Addressed.* This book addresses needs and situations of the elderly which lead to anxieties, other forms of emotional and physical distress, and dilemmas. These needs and situations, which will be discussed in more detail later on, prominently include the following, although they are not restricted to them:

a. Prolonged or unusual grief reactions. Personal losses are the most common form of distress among the elderly. Recovery can often be sufficiently aided by some pastoral care and self-help groups of the bereaved. But prolonged or otherwise unusual grief is unfortunately all too frequent among the elderly, especially among widows and widowers. Although pastoral counseling may not be all that is needed to aid these persons, it may often be useful as a way to start the resolution process, sometimes to effect it, or to follow up on any specific treatment.

b. Spiritual questions with personal coloration. Many common questions usually regarded as spiritual in character can most suitably be addressed by means of education—such as the nature of the life journey and what happens when we die. But most such questions come in the shape of yearnings, murmurings, and fears which have idiosyncratic features of a personal nature. These can often be addressed through pastoral counseling.

c. Relationships with children. Much has been written for middle-aged children about the relationships they have with their parents. Little or nothing has been written either for aging parents about how to get along with their children, or for their caregivers, but these relationships are a frequent source of anxiety. Well-meaning attempts on the part of children to care for their parents are often felt as restrictions on freedom and integrity, leading to refusals to discuss the future and sometimes to outright hostility. The difficulties inherent in the process of negotiating these shoals in family relationships can be greatly mitigated by pastoral counseling.

d. Prevention of clinical depression or as an adjunct to recovery from depression. Depression is a debilitating and painful disease which is widespread in our society, particularly among the elderly. While, except in its milder forms, it cannot usually be successfully treated by counseling alone, the precipitating factors often can be addressed. Therefore, early recognition is a key. Pastoral counseling may also be useful during recovery from depression as a way of increasing the meaning and comfort of living, and hence as a preventative of recurrence.

e. Interpersonal/institutional rejection. Senior citizens are frequently living alone and have no family to turn to when they experience rejection by other persons who are important to them either because of close relationships, or because the persons represent groups, such as church groups, social clubs, and even Senior Citizen Centers, that are important. Hence, these rejections cut more deeply and have longer lasting effects. Pastoral counseling can mitigate these effects and help point the way toward a less vulnerable future.

f. Vocational questions. It is a mistake to think of the elderly as having no vocation, as if retirement from occupation is the end of vocational life. Indeed, vocational questions often haunt the elderly. They often search for vocational meaning in leisure without finding it. Volunteering provides at least a partial answer for many, but feelings of something lacking frequently remain. Vocation is fundamentally a matter of the spirit and can be focally addressed through pastoral counseling.

g. Marital difficulties. Marital difficulties may beset long-enduring marriages because of changed circumstances and/or the changed health status of one or both partners. They may also, and perhaps more frequently, occur in late-life marriages with even more devastation, since hopes have been high. Marital problems are perhaps more likely to lead the elderly to seek pastoral counseling than any other difficulty.

h. Decisions faced by the elderly regarding their more elderly parents. Increasingly, persons in their 60s and 70s have the care of their parents who are in their 80s, 90s and 100s. Frequently they need help in considering the options for care which they may have. Often disastrous mistakes are made, resulting in both the overburdening of the caregivers and the discomfort of the aged parents. Pastoral counseling can help in sorting out the internal cognitive/emotive factors and the external options.

4. *Conclusion.* All these needs and situations involve the future in some way, so the question of anthropology, of what it is to be human and to be aging, pervades all. Different styles of counseling are appropriate for different persons and questions, and these will be discussed in chapter 9. Now we turn to the cultural background in North America and its influence upon the processes of aging, and then to the focal question of theological anthropology.

Chapter 2

The Cultural Situation

The rejection of the elderly by our culture is too well-known to rehearse it in detail here. This rejection is now changing to some extent because the sheer numbers of the aging population have begun to affect marketing strategies—60-year-old women now appear on the cover of *Vogue*. But the prevailing attitude persists, for it is deeply rooted in western social psychology and history. I shall discuss some of the factors within these perspectives which I think are most pertinent to this current study.

1. *Social Psychology*. In the middle and upper middle class, and to a lesser extent in other social classes, the capacity to change in some direction deemed positive is pivotal for the preservation of identity and the maintenance and enhancement of self-esteem. This capacity is manifested in vocational striving—including both occupations and childrearing, but not excluding other pursuits sometimes mislabeled avocations. Key manifestations in our culture related to the capacity to change are revivalism, psychotherapy, self-help groups, financial gain, and accrual of power. The elderly, with some exceptions, are not perceived, either by others or by themselves, as able to participate in these modes of activity and existence. Rather, they are perceived as too slow to keep up, too addled to know how to participate, and sometimes as "having an untreatable disease,"[1] that is, old age.

To protect themselves from these perceptions the elderly fiercely maintain their independence. Individualism has been under fire in our society in recent years, notably from Robert Bellah and his colleagues in *Matters of the Heart*,[2] where it is depicted as a threat to the common good. A positive side of individualism is that it provides freedom from many entangle-

9

ments of family and tribe, and it is this freedom that the elderly seek to protect. Unhappily, they pay too dear a price for it by shunning opportunities for personal help that they frequently need.[3] At the same time the society as a whole resists offering them those opportunities. Gurian and Cantor note that community mental-health centers were giving a low priority to older people in the late 1970s, to cite one instance in an area closely related to pastoral counseling.[4] They believe that, in addition to the well-known emphasis on youth in our culture, another factor in this resistance to offering help to the elderly is that mental-health workers identify the elderly with their parents. They then avoid relationships that may trigger painful conflicts.[5]

Thus, many of the elderly are caught in a psychosocial bind not of their own making. They have survived as exemplary products of a culture which has emphasized independence and individualism, but in their advanced years they need to accept personal and other forms of assistance without feelings of shame and personal failure—a thing very hard for many to do. Continuity of character, and hence personal integrity, is often at stake. They experience cultural rejection as a dark reward for upholding the values of the culture, and accept help, which may be reluctantly offered, only as a last resort. For those born around 1920, whom we shall call the "cohort of 1920," as well as for those born earlier, all forms of counseling and psychotherapy suggest that the recipients of such help are crazy. This state of affairs results in withdrawal from society for some, and in physical and mental deterioration in some degree for many, as was sketched in chapter 1.

For some of the elderly this state of affairs is mitigated by multiple social contacts both within their own age group and across the span of life. In *Invisible Lives: Social Worlds of the Aged*, David R. Unruh discusses the various social worlds in which the elderly live, defining social world as ". . . an extremely large, highly permeable, amorphous, and spatially transcendent, form of social organization wherein actors are linked cognitively through shared perspectives arising out of common channels of communication."[6] This definition by its scope includes distant "worlds" of media contact only, as well as those with whom the elderly have face-to-face contacts. Both kinds may enrich the lives of the elderly.

2. *History.* The immediate psychosocial factors impinging on the elderly have, of course, historical antecedents, both remote and proximate, which have played a role in their development. In the Decalogue, the Hebrews were commanded to honor their fathers and mothers, with the assurance of long life in the land of promise(Ex 20:12). This injunction was reflected throughout the Old Testament, though with varying emphases. J. Gordon Harris, who has made a careful study of the topic, tells us that, while this attitude toward the elderly was prevalent throughout the ancient Middle East, it was intensified in Israel, because of the experience of the Hebrews with Yahweh, the God of justice who led them out of Egypt when they were weak and oppressed, and who thus manifested a concern for all who were especially vulnerable.[7] The repeated injunctions in the Old Testament to honor and care for the aged seem to be a clear indication that the Hebrews were not always inclined to do so.

In the New Testament the picture is rather different. The synoptic gospels and the main Pauline epistles have a heavy emphasis on the dawning of the new age and a relative silence regarding the elderly, with occasional negative comments which identify the old with the "old age."[8] As time progressed, the literature reflected more of the theological understanding of Judaism toward the elderly, as shown in Colossians and Ephesians, the Johannine literature, and the pastoral and general epistles, although this is in some tension with the still present emphasis on the "new age."[9] This respect and concern for the elderly was reinforced by Roman law in the early church and in Judaism of the early Christian era.[10]

Although remote in time, the support for a positive theology of aging—including social support systems, community and self-esteem of the elderly, the capacity of the elderly for learning and contributing to the life of the community—offered by the Jewish and Christian scriptures is a background factor of great importance, even in a society grown relatively illiterate regarding scripture. For beneath the surface of the culture lie the residuals of scriptural injunction and aphorism which can be tapped to raise the consciousness of the society about the needs of the aging.

By the end of the Middle Ages respect and esteem for the elderly had markedly eroded. That preeminent figure of the Renaissance, Shakespeare, drawing on medieval sources, repeatedly depicts old men as fools. Lear, Falstaff, and Polonius are all foolish men, even though the last named spouted aphorisms which have been rightly regarded as wisdom for others— "This above all: to thine own self be true, and it must follow, as the night the day, Thou canst not then be false to any man."[11]

The humanism begun in the Renaissance and brought to full flower in the Enlightenment improved the status of the elderly in western culture, but the coming of the industrial age with its emphasis on productivity (skill plus speed) again moved the perception of the elderly in the direction of the scarcely human in the early decades of the twentieth century, especially in areas where agriculture had been supplanted by industry.

The influence of the Protestant Reformed tradition on the shaping of culture in North America is well-known and I shall not describe it here. Brought to these shores by English Puritans, Scottish and English Presbyterians, Dutch Reformed settlers, and French Huguenots, this influence resulted in a culture-Calvinism, when mixed with other elements in the culture in the nineteenth and early twentieth centuries, not envisioned by Calvin and his immediate successors. Phrases such as "the Protestant work ethic," and "capitalist striving" are among the elements associated with this influence, along with a fierce independence (alluded to earlier), and a characterological shape marked sometimes by rigidity, but also by rectitude in personal and business dealings, including verbal commitments. Those currently in the population of the elderly may be the last to be markedly shaped by culture-Calvinism, but many are so shaped, even if their familial roots were outside the Reformed tradition.

This sketch of some key epochs in western culture, and in North America in particular, shows that the pattern has not always been that of denigration of the elderly, but recent centuries do not, on the whole, offer a positive picture of their status.

To be sure, their numbers were comparatively few until the present generation. Moreover, their attitudes toward their heirs and successors were not always exemplary, as Lear offers symbolic testimony.

The situation of the present generation (or more precisely, *two* generations of elderly) is clearly influenced by the history which preceded it, but also by events contemporary to its own life. To these we now turn.

3. *The Immediate Cultural Heritage.* All those persons over 60 years of age, except those in very affluent economic circumstances, who were reared in the United States and Canada experienced the direct effects of the Great Depression of the 1930s. Some experienced these effects as children and adolescents, others as adults, but the great majority experienced those years as a time of anxiety, fear and uncertainty, if not outright poverty and hunger, which have left scars on many, if not most of the elderly. They tend to be overly cautious about money and any other matters which they feel impinge upon their economic situation. In some instances this attitude results in their failure to spend money on their own needs, which in turn results in health and welfare problems which could have been prevented. In many instances it precipitates conflict between the elderly and their children, who see more clearly the need to expend financial resources on health care, and sometimes even nutrition.

The culture-Calvinism discussed above combined with the lingering effects of the Great Depression to produce a generation of the elderly who have survived in part by overcoming difficulties imposed by the culture through maintaining personal independence insofar as they could, and by a degree of suspicion of those who might perceive them to be in need. They tend to seek help only when they feel they have no alternative.

An added factor in the resistance of the elderly to pastoral counseling and other forms of personal helping is their sense that, to engage in that kind of process, is an admission of mental illness or craziness. The cohort of 1920 came of age in a time before modes of helping that employed a dynamic psychological perspective were at all widespread, and their associations with such helping are often still to mental hospitals, or to put it in terms they were familiar with in their youth—to insane asylums. These feelings are present in both men and women, although more intense in some men because of the perceived threat to their masculinity. It is hard for them to see that allowing for a degree of interdependence is a better adaptation in later years than the independence and individualism—the "standing on their own two feet," that got them there.

This attitude is less prevalent in those now joining the ranks of senior citizens, some of whom were children during World War II, and adolescents in the postwar period when the mental health movement became a widespread phenomenon in our society. They are more ready to open themselves to relationships which they perceive as potentially helpful.

4. *Conclusion.* The culture contains a mix of attitudes toward the elderly comprised of biblical injunctions to honor one's parents, Judeo-Christian and Enlightenment ideas of social responsibility for those on the margins of society, notions of the foolishness and churlishness of older people which stem from the Middle Ages (and, of course, which sometimes are embodied in living persons), and industrial age perceptions that the elderly are worn out and unproductive.

The elderly themselves partake to some degree of all these attitudes as well, and in addition, possess a strong sense of their own selfhood as survivors of tough times—a selfhood potentially vulnerable to threats from a culture they may have reason to suspect. Hence, they are self-protective through a sense of independence developed as participants in culture-Calvinism.

This sense of independence in reality is a kind of pseudo-independence that is costly to them. Pastoral counseling can reduce these costs and address many issues which lie hidden behind the facade of independence. But those who would offer it must take full account of the strength of the character defenses which protect the elderly from unwanted intrusion. Approaches must be cultivated gently in most instances and the level of trust built high before they will open their personal worlds enough to receive the help they need.

Chapter 3

The Elderly as Human Beings

1. *The Importance of a Model.* As indicated in the first chapter, one of the obstacles facing anyone who intends to do counseling with older adults, is that the models of human beings which have been influential in our culture are, for the most part, young adult models. At first glance this point may seem to be of little practical significance for the counselor, but I hope to show that it is of great importance.

When one assumes that human beings are characterized primarily by quick response time, driving ambition, high levels of sexual energy, and a struggle to define themselves both in relation to and distinct from families of origin and their own families created by marriage or other relational matrices, then older adults do not fit this paradigm of human being. Even at their most active and healthy, they do not appear to be able to meet the criteria implied in these phrases. They are not very quick, as their psychomotor systems have slowed down. They do have ambitions, but for most these are not as consuming as they formerly were. They often possess sexual energy well into the ninth decade, but it is not as central to their lives as it once was. Loving and working are important, as Freud is reputed to have said they were, but for the elderly they are no longer sufficient to define their goals of human life. The tension between independence and relatedness remains for them, but it does not so focally concern the individual, as Robert Kegan has persuasively argued, that it does through the first three decades of life.[1] Erik Erikson's emphasis on the maintenance of integrity previously acquired is a necessary element, but new directions which require the expansion of once-formed identities or their reshaping may also be in order for the elderly.

So, unless we are willing to consign the elderly to some

shadowy quasi-human limbo, we must find an anthropological model large and accurate enough to encompass them. Otherwise, we shall continue to be nagged by a sense of futility, and doubt that our efforts at counseling older persons are worthwhile. Pastoral counselors must regard the elderly as fully human, even though their embodiment of the characteristics of humanity may be different from that of younger generations.

2. *Existing Models of Aging.* K. Warner Schaie has stated that most persons designing experimental or quasi-experimental research dealing with questions of aging assume one of three models of aging: irreversible decrement, stability, or decrement with compensation.[2] It seems to me that these three models do underlie, not only research, but the thinking of professionals seeking to help those who are aging. All of them refer backward in time to previous levels of functioning which are thought to be superior to or essentially the same as present levels. As such, none will serve my purposes in this book in a complete way. Nevertheless, each serves to highlight some features of the aging process which must be taken into account in any model which can be developed. There are undeniable decrements, or losses of function, in the aging process, and also compensations for these losses. We shall examine these processes in three areas of mental functioning—memory, intelligence, and the emotions. Then we shall look at them in physiology, with emphasis on the immune system, and finally, in the area of ambition. These will be looked at in relation to phases of the aging process.

3. *Functioning of the Elderly.*

a. Phases of aging. These are phases and not stages which must somehow be got through, since they are not absolutely discrete, but rather merge into one another and overlap. Hence, the time frames proposed are only approximations, and may change as culture, nutrition, health practices, and personality development enable longer active lives. Some time frames are necessary in any approach to the study of aging, since the total time in this so-called "stage" may be up to 45 or more years (55 to 100+), making it far longer than any other conventional stage in the life cycle. The Social Security system, following the lead of Bismarck, who inaugurated the first social security system in nineteenth-century Germany, designates 65 as the age at which retirement, and hence, "aging" begins, in the minds of many. However, many persons are retiring at 55 or younger, and thus join their older peers in significant respects of their lives. Thus we can say that the first phase of "aging" is from about 55 to about 75—"the young old." Persons in this age group have continuity with middle age in many respects, although they may suffer some decrements in others, and experience the onset of major health problems.

The second phase, which may be called "the middle old," lasts from about 75 to 85. In this phase some former elements in life-style will likely have to be given up, and hopefully replaced by others more suited to the physiological and psychological resources of the individual. If sheer "activity" is the measure of the viability of life-style, however, those in this age group may appear to be failing, for they often become less "active" in any obvious sense, and more disengaged from institutions.

At this point some comment on the long-running controversy about "disengagement theory" seems to be in order. In 1961 Cumming and Henry published a study of older people called *Growing Old,* in which they advocated a theory of aging as progressive disengagement from social and institutional involvements.[3] This theory challenged the then prevailing (and still prevalent) theory of activity, which viewed old age as a continuity of middle age which optimally is characterized by continuing, and even increasing, activity involving institutions and social relationships. In our time there has been a growing recognition that both theories are at least partly right when differences in personality, social situation, and physical resources are taken into account.

The age group of the "middle old" presents us with the clearest picture of why this is so. Persons in this age group must make choices about continuing activity and relative disengagement on an ongoing basis. Depending upon factors which are unique to the individual, either choice may be the right one at any given time. Community expectations based upon one theory or the other, particularly upon activity theory, may make it hard to make the appropriate choice of disengagement. But appropriate activity should never be discouraged. Hence, we can see the importance of respecting the core of both theories when seeking to aid persons to make such choices.

Continuity theory, which emphasizes the use of long acquired traits and skills to make adaptive changes in new circumstances may be best able to account for the changes required in the phase of life here called "middle old." "To the extent that change builds upon, and has links to the person's past, change is a part of continuity."[4] This vision is similar to activity theory in building upon the past, but is more evolutionary in its emphasis upon adaptation than the more homeostatic activity theory, which emphasizes carrying activity patterns of middle age into old age. Whether continuity theory is fully able to account for the phenomenon of attempts to use learned behaviors in circumstances where these behaviors are not appropriate, as sometimes occurs in this age group, is open to question.

The last age group, "the old old," covers the age span from about 85 to about 100. With this group disengagement theory seems to have its best fit, but there are many individuals who remain actively engaged in community affairs throughout much of this period in their lives, contributing through talents developed over a lifetime, or through newly acquired knowledge and skills. A woman of 94 plays piano accompaniment for group singing, another continues to participate in garden club activities. Death lies inevitably at the end of this phase, but may come either with relative suddenness or more slowly at the end of decline.

The question of longevity arises, of course, when discussing this phase of life. Biologist Takashi Makinodan confidently tells us that the human life span is about 110 years, and that it is not susceptible to environmental manipulation.[5] From time to time the press reports findings with animal or human studies that appear to contradict this presumed limitation, and which suggest much higher theoretical limitations. However, for the present and the immediate future it seems wise to me to accept Makinodan's limit, based as it is upon careful biological assessment. The upper limit of aging is finite, and although we can expect more and more persons to attain the age of 100 or more through improved nutrition, medical care and other environmental factors, it is unlikely that many will exceed the age of 110. This assumption provides us with a realistic sense of finitude when attempting to assess the potential longevity of older persons, even though we may be able to look forward to improved physiology through hormonal modification and other induced changes within these limits (e.g., "Human Growth Hormone Reverses Effects of Aging," *New York Times*, July 5, 1990).

It is well-known that many persons do not fit this age phase scheme. Some seem to be greatly aged by 60, with slowness of motor functions, speech, and intellectual performance. Such early decrements seem best attributed to environmental stress and the individual's response to it, though genetic bases cannot be ruled out.

b. Memory. Memory is a crucial factor in virtually all human functioning. Clearly, it is in forms of counseling which rely in a significant way on the recall of the past—that is, in most forms of counseling. There is widespread belief that the memories of the elderly are failing—a belief that impedes the undertaking of counseling with them. Hence, we must examine rather carefully the state of existing knowledge about memory in the aging—a state which, unfortunately for our purposes, is far from crystal clear.

Traditionally, theorists have distinguished between short and long-term memory, with every span more than 20 or 30 seconds being classified as long term. Verbal items were thought to have been encoded acoustically in short-term memory, and lost either by decay or by active displacement by other auditory signals.

Long-term memory was thought to have no capacity limitations. Encoding, or recording, took place semantically, that is, by verbal cues, written or oral, and forgetting was attributed either to interference by new encoding or to loss of accessibility.[6] The learning model was that of a simple stimulus/response event.

Fergus I. M. Craik, building upon the work of Waugh and Norman, challenged this model, noting that long and short-term functioning were not discrete and that the phenomena could be better accounted for by a three-stage information processing model. In this model, sensory encoding results in primary memory which may be retained by rehearsal (short-term store) and then (possibly) transmitted to secondary memory (long-term store). These processes are sequential and not discrete.[7]

On the basis of this model, Craik seriously questioned the prevailing view among theorists that the normal elderly do have short-term memory capacity but are deficient in long-term memory. (I note that the theorists have not upheld the cultural view that memory of remote events by the elderly is unimpaired.) He did uphold the view that short-term (primary memory) is unimpaired unless division of attention or reorganization of material is involved.[8] But he cautioned that primary memory is affected by secondary memory, which tends to penalize the elderly in divided attention situations.[9] The elderly are less accurate in recalling details of discrete events in the past than are young adults, but their recall markedly improves when they are able to organize their recall by means of key concepts, such as watershed events like high school graduation, which control a hierarchy of memories.[10] Memories of childhood events are distorted by repeated recall and rehearsal, but are nevertheless present.[11]

Recently, theorists using a multiple memory systems model have tended to support the view that the elderly are less memory impaired than had been previously thought. They postulate "episodic" memory for events, "semantic" memory for knowledge and facts, and "implicit" memory for skills one can exercise automatically, such as how to hit a golf ball properly—which may survive even severe strokes. Only episodic memory is thought by these theorists to be impaired. This impairment is due to interference by recent events, and can be retrieved under some circumstances. This kind of memory deals with yesterday's events as well as those in the remote past, and hence is prominent in the lives of the elderly who may have misplaced items in daily use, such as car keys. I note that younger persons also have this trouble, as the varied reports of eyewitnesses to accidents testify. Says David Mitchell, a psychologist at Southern Methodist University, "The idea that memory inevitably deteriorates as you age came from studies that only tested one kind of memory. Now we see that there are multiple memory systems, and they each hold up differently as you age."[12]

We can see from the foregoing sketches that the last word about memory has not been said, since thinking continues to evolve among experimenters and theorists. Even the basic model for memory is not settled, as we have seen in the leap from Craik's sequential model to the multiple model employed by Mitchell and his colleagues. Nevertheless, there seems to be agreement that the elderly are not necessarily irreversibly handicapped by memory loss, if they are not also beset by chemical and/or structural impairment. This converging view is supported by the psychoanalytic postulate that forgetting at all ages is, in most instances, a function of interference of recall, rather than a loss of memory trace. Further anecdotal evidence is seen in the ability of persons in their 70s and 80s to complete college degrees in an extension program at Arizona State University and other schools, since such a program demands both the acquisition of new learning as well as recall of a diversity of material.[13] From playing bridge and chess with some elderly persons at a local senior citizen center I found that, although some apparent memory decrements were observed, one man of 89 had the ability to remember every card that had been played![14]

I conclude that memory deficiencies do not constitute an overriding reason why counseling should not be done with the elderly. Counselors will have to be patient and often offer memory-jogging cues to the elderly, but these behaviors are frequently requisite in doing counseling with persons of any age. With respect to memory the elderly are human, but perhaps a little more so, in the sense that their failings may be more frequent.

c. Intelligence. Just as they have been thought to have lost memory, the elderly have also been thought to have lost intellectual power. Although the retention of intellectual faculties is not as crucial as memory for our purposes in this book, some comment is in order. According to a report in *The New York Times* in 1984, older people do lose some ability in the area of fluid intelligence which is employed in discerning relationships among abstractions, as in mathematics and physics, or in chess. (Some support for this last point came from playing chess with persons at the senior citizen center.) However, they do not lose ability in the area of crystallized intelligence, or the ability to make judgments on the basis of accumulated information. This ability, traditionally called wisdom, may, in fact increase into the ninth decade of life. Crystallized intelligence in the elderly does depend upon the development of this capacity earlier in life.

A. E. David Schonfield has stated that the elderly are much poorer acquirers of classical conditioned responses than younger persons, but he also indicated that we lack sufficient studies to state such points definitively.[15] This point does suggest that the elderly tend to rely more upon previously acquired knowledge than new knowledge, unless strongly motivated toward new learning. Such new learning frequently is a part of the counseling process, although how large a part this will be varies. In any case, motivation and patience will frequently be needed.

d. Emotions. It is a widespread observation that the strength of the emotions markedly diminishes in later life. Although I have no reason to dispute this truism, it is an exaggeration to say, as does A. E. David Schonfeld, "Don't expect great happiness or unhappiness from the aged."[16] Except perhaps for the very old, the elderly are capable of experiencing great joy and sorrow, for these emotional states accrue from complex interactions of cognitive and emotive sets which, when combined with expectations met, exceeded, or dashed, produce strong emotional responses.

Recently, researchers may have thrown some light on the relative diminishment of fear and anxiety in later life. Focusing on the middle years between 40 and 60, these researchers found a loss of cells in the locus coeroleus, a tiny part of the brain located at the base of the brain, which is the seat of the neural alarm system. The locus coeroleus also produces norepinephrine, a neurotransmitter, according to the same report. A lack of norepinephrine is widely thought to be a factor in depression, one of the major plagues of the aging, which will be treated in some detail in chapter 6 dealing with indicators for pastoral counseling.[17]

Here we can note that physiological bases for emotional diminishment, especially of the negative emotions, are beginning to be uncovered. I must stress that these emotions are diminished, not extinguished, and that the elderly are still capable of anger, anxiety, and fear, even though politicians addressing gatherings of the elderly are sometimes astonished at their politeness! Anxieties are frequently combined with cognitive elements in the elderly to produce worry, fretfulness, and to present a mildly irritated personality to the world.

e. Sexuality. Despite widespread belief to the contrary, there is no evidence that the capacity for sexual enjoyment disappears or markedly diminishes well into the ninth decade of life. Males require greater stimulation after about age 50, but do not experience impotence (failure to attain an erection) because of the aging process as such. Rather, impotence results from psychological or physiological disturbances (or both) which may accompany aging, such as prostate difficulties.[18] Less attention has been paid to women because of the perceived importance of male potency and its complexities in sexual relations. Some women do respond to androgen hormones with enhanced sexual interest and response, though men do not.[19]

Heart attack and stroke seldom occur during sexual intercourse, although these are major fears. Women are not sexually disabled by diabetes, as are men. Testosterone is not now believed to be as large a factor in male potency as it formerly was.[20] Hence, the decline in testosterone levels in aging men may have no great effect. Sexual activity is thought to decline for both sexes, and sexual interest on the part of women (but not on the part of men), perhaps due to widowhood and lack of opportunity.[21]

We can see from the foregoing that many of the sexual difficulties encountered by the elderly are due to poor information about their sexual abilities. Although this is obviously a sensitive area, all the more so because of sexual inhibitions likely to be present in this age group, which had its sex "education" in the 1930s and before, counseling can do a great deal to alleviate sexual fears and frustrations among the elderly. The key is sufficient motivation to enter counseling and the ability of the counselor to create an atmosphere of comfort in which these matters can be fruitfully discussed.

f. The immune system. For some time researchers have been pointing to links between affective/behavioral states, particularly those associated with bereavement, and deficiencies in the immune system. In a relatively early study, Bartrop and his associates found that 26 bereaved spouses studied two to six weeks after the death of a spouse showed a decrease in response of lymphocytes and reduction in B and T cell function.[22] That the decrease in lymphocyte response was due to bereavement was confirmed by Schieifer *et al.* in a longitudinal study of 20 spouses of women with breast carcinoma that proved fatal. Response levels returned to normal during the second six-month period in the first year of bereavement in most spouses.[23]

These findings are of particular importance for the aging because of the frequency of losses, and the great importance of the maintenance of an intact immune system. The immune system can be maintained essentially intact well into the tenth decade, as clinical studies have shown.[24] Although not all the precise effects of deficits in the immune system are known, its general role in the prevention of cancers and diseases caused by invasive organisms is well-established.

The operations of the immune system are complex, and its details need not concern us here. A few basic points can be of assistance, however, in understanding the research most pertinent to those involved in the counseling of the elderly. The immune system consists of B (or humoral) cells, so-called because they were first isolated in the "bursa of Fabricus" in birds, and T cells, so-called because they are matured in the thymus. These cells function in complex interaction with one another, with B cells operating in relation to the humors, or fluids, of the body, and T cells operating in relation to the structural cells. In addition there are other cell types involved in the immune system: monocytes, macrophages, mast cells, and neutrophils. Both B and T cells are thought to be manufactured in the bone marrow, and both are called lymphocytes.[25]

The immune system provides protection against a vast array of antigens, or foreign substances, with each cell targeting a specific antigen. Humoral cells primarily protect the body from infections by encapsulated bacteria such as pneumonococci, and T cells provide viral and fungial immunity, protection against intracellular bacteria infection, and probably neoplastic (or cancer) surveillance.[26]

In some instances malfunction of the immune system causes disease. Risk of three of these are known to increase with age. These are certain infections which may occur in relation to cancer and other diseases, the autoimmune diseases (diseases caused by the immune system), rheumatoid arthritis and autoimmune thyroiditis, and amyloidosis, a starch-like degeneration of tissue observed in 50% of males over 70.[27]

Although many forms of stress may temporarily suppress the immune system, recovery is usual after a few days when the stressor is removed.[28] However, severity of depression, thought to be the most significant element in bereavement related to immune deficiency, was found to be related to decreased mitogen levels in a careful study carried out by Schleifer and his colleagues. Mitogen production is a result of lymphocyte stimulation, hence their conclusion that depression is a factor in the suppression of the immune system.[29]

The prevention of depression and other forms of stress becomes a high priority in the pastoral care and counseling of the elderly when these findings are taken into account. Not only is depression a very debilitating and painful experience in itself, but it may well contribute to the vulnerability of the elderly to lethal physical diseases such as cancer and major infections. R. Scott Sullender, in his *Losses in Later Life: a New Way of Walking with God*, has helpfully detailed the multiple losses which later life often brings—loss of youth, loss of family, loss of parents, loss of work, loss of spouse, loss of health and loss of identity, as well as others.[30] The weight of these contributes heavily to the tendency of the elderly toward depression.

In recent years bereavement, the most conspicuous and often the most painful, loss has received much more attention than it did formerly, and many communities provide groups and other forms of support for the bereaved, which are often effective for those who can reach out and use them. Some persons are not inclined, or perhaps not able to reach out, however, and these people require special concern. The particular uses of pastoral counseling in bereavement will be treated in chapter 6.

g. The nervous system. The nervous system suffers undeniable losses over a long lifetime. According to Raymond Adams, all the neurons are present at birth and cannot be regenerated (even though most other cells can be regenerated). Losses of neurons occur over a lifetime, sometimes by small and hardly noticed strokes. Average loss of brain weight is 5 percent at age 70, 10 percent at age 80, and 20 percent at age 90. These are the averages of all persons, of course, and mean that many persons experience less brain-weight loss. Neurofibillary tangles characteristic of Alzheimer's disease sufferers are thought to be caused by abnormalities in protein metabolism.[31]

The functional meaning of most of these structural losses is unclear (as Adams, for instance, acknowledges), since functional intellectual processes continue at relatively unimpeded levels, as was shown earlier in this section, and neurophysical motor responses also continue, albeit at a slower rate. Nor is it clear that most neuronal loss occurs after the age of 65, although brain-weight loss indicates that some of it does. Nevertheless, we must acknowledge that these structural losses occur, and take them into account in both thinking about and in trying to aid the elderly.

Much more clear are the effects of sensory-neural losses, especially loss or diminishment of hearing and sight. But these diminishments can be compensated for to a large extent, due to the heavy investment of our culture in help for the blind especially, but to a lesser extent in help for the deaf. Deafness is a particularly difficult handicap for older people, since everyday communication with family members depends upon hearing. Hence, every effort should be made to compensate for hearing loss.

h. Ambition. Ambition does not seem at first glance to belong in this series of functional discussions. As an attribution of a person or a trait of character, it is clearly not of the same order as the immune system or even the somewhat more elusive emotions. Yet, the level of functioning of ambition—the motivation to attain some goal or to participate in some endeavor—is a key issue in understanding the elderly. Often they are depicted as being without ambition, or with such a low level of ambition that it is not observable, either by themselves or by others. Although the level of drive (used here in the broad sense of intensely organized energy) is lower in older persons, this fact does not mean that they are without ambition.

There is no evidence that exploratory drive, characteristic of human beings and many animals diminishes with age as such. But homeostatic mechanisms, regulated by the hypothalamus, do slow down; novelty is not as much sought. Risk taking diminishes, as does problem solving behavior in which the pain of effort seems not to be justified by the probable result. There is frequently more cognitive dissonance, as the culture moves on without the elderly on board, resulting in their withdrawal.[32]

Despite these negative factors affecting ambition, there is much evidence that many elderly persons make rather dramatic adaptational changes at about retirement age, embarking on new business ventures or new careers, while others continue in the vocational path already trod, albeit with appropriate changes. Women show some tendencies to focus more upon personal satisfaction than upon nurturance in later life.[33] In one study more than 50 percent of the elderly were found to plan for the future.[34]

While it is sometimes hard for the elderly to admit to themselves or others that they have ambitions, since they, in many instances, have learned to live a life of low resources and low expectations, these unmet and unacknowledged ambitions can cause trouble. They gnaw at the sense of well-being, and undermine contentment. Although it cannot be said that all older persons have unacknowledged ambitions, many do, and it is important for counselors to surface these and take them into account in attempting to assist them. Some have acknowledged ambitions, which may be realistic or unrealistic, and these need to be discussed. The counselor should never assume that the elderly are lacking in ambition without careful assessment.

4. *Summary.* The various functional dimensions of the lives of the elderly discussed in this section clearly indicate that none of the three models of aging—the decrement model, the stability model, or the decrement with compensation model, is entirely adequate. Some facts fit each model, but none can accommodate all the facts. There are some decrements in the areas of memory, intelligence, emotional response, neuronal structure, and motivation for high risk endeavors (although some of these begin long before age 65). Relative stability in the immune system is necessary for survival into old age, as it is in the various homeostatic mechanisms of the body, even though these may be slowed by the influence of the hypothalamus. Compensations may be observed in mundane behaviors, such as wearing more sweaters, and in more complex operations, such as the use of wisdom, expanded vocabulary, and experience to compensate for lack of mental swiftness. Some decrements may even be said to be beneficial, such as the reduction in the power of the negative emotions.

A model of the human being is needed which can take these facts into account, but which is not based upon any one cluster of them. I believe that enough has been said to make the point that an older person is not just a decremented version of a young person—even one with compensations. Rather, we need a model which can accommodate adult human beings of all ages, but which is not based on the phenomena offered by any one age group. Such a model would enable us to examine the elderly and the help which may be offered to them "without prejudice." It would also enable us to study humans across age groups more fruitfully, and make a contribution to the study of other age groups by setting them in a sufficiently broad and, hopefully, accurate context.

In the next chapter I shall present a model human functioning based primarily upon theological, psychological and experiential sources which, I hope, will be shown to possess the characteristics of comprehensiveness, analytical potency, and heuristic usefulness required for the study of older persons and their relationships. This model may be called a self-spirit model, as it centers on the interaction of these important dimensions of human life, when they are properly understood.

Chapter 4

An Age-Inclusive Model of Human Being: Spirit and Self

In the first section of this chapter a sketch of the model focused upon the relationships between spirit and self will be presented. First, these terms will be discussed separately with some attention to their histories and attempts to describe their contemporary usage and meaning in the model. Then the model, based on their interaction, will be described. For a more detailed presentation of the thinking lying behind the model, the reader is referred to two articles published in *Pastoral Psychology* in 1986 and 1990.[1]

1. *Spirit.* Anyone wishing to use the term spirit to denote something specific must reckon with the fact that the term has 22 meanings in *Webster's New International Dictionary* (Second Edition, Unabridged). This seeming diffuseness of meaning can be accounted for in large measure by two rather different strands of meaning (which, to be sure, overlap to some extent).

The first is derived mainly from the Bible, in which terms in both Hebrew and Greek that mean "life" or "breath" are usually translated "spirit." The Latin word from which our term spirit is derived, *spiritus*, has a similar meaning. This strand of meaning carries the weight of the biblical tradition, and shows affinities with animistic cultures which view all of nature as pervaded with life, as in primitive Roman culture. A contemporary variant on this theme is the use of the term spirit to advertise young women's clothing, automobiles, and cigarettes (a dubious use).

The second is derived primarily from the tradition of idealistic philosophy in western thought, which was inspired initially by Plato, but which found its fullest expression in the

German idealism of the nineteenth century. In this strand "spirit" has a decidedly mentalistic cast, and is often virtually synonymous with mind, sometimes thought of as a property of the cosmos.

In some instances "spirit" may show influences of both traditions. The use of the term synonymous with "ghost" is derived from animism but is reinforced by the body-mind dualism associated with some strands of idealism. When used to refer to the characteristic emotional bent or temper of a person or a group, it reflects the underlying life-motif but with a mentalistic flavor. A group of terms found in pharmacology and alcohol distillation are derived from uses in alchemy. In this model I shall be sticking mainly to the cluster of biblical meanings and their derivatives, as these are the ones at the core of modern Christian anthropology.

In the Hebrew scriptures, spirit (*ruach*) is characteristic both of God as creator of humanity and the human being whose spirit is the result of the divine inbreathing. ". . . then the Lord formed man of dust from the ground, and breathed into his nostrils the breath of life; and man became a living being" (Gen 2:7). The term "being" was in former times translated "soul." Spirit is the special gift of life conferred by the divine spirit; soul is the resulting structure of human existence which belongs to human beings in a sense which spirit does not. At death soul dissolves, and spirit is taken away by God whose gift it was (Ps 104:29), and returns to God (Eccl 12:7).

This same structure is also found in the New Testament, except that the emphasis is now upon the soteriological function of the divine spirit (*pneuma*). The writings of Paul have held a normative position for western theology, and there the indwelling of the spirit of Christ is taken as decisive for salvation. The new life in Christ presupposes the original life created by the divine spirit.[2] Human beings have body and soul, but they partake of spirit, in a sense "on loan" from their creator, which provides power of motion and direction in human life, and its fundamental connection to the divine life in creation, renewal, and reunion.

Spirit is the basis of such lofty human characteristics and aspirations as truth, art, and freedom. But it is also found in passion, confusion, grief, and destructive intentions and acts. It partakes of all the ambiguities of human life.

The human spirit is, then, the human form of life itself. *It provides intensity of motion and direction toward other beings and toward a vision of the future.* Other beings include especially other human beings and God. The future is centered on a central purpose.

2. *Self.* Like spirit, the term "self" is in widespread use in the English-speaking world, and does not possess a single precise meaning. In most common use is the *phenomenal* self, the one that refers to the felt awareness of one's own personhood. This self is both continuous over time—its "sameness," and designates our distinctiveness from other persons—our identity or "ownness." Both sameness and ownness poles of the term go back to its beginnings in the Middle Ages when it was used only as a reflexive intensifer to distinguish one person from another, as in the phrase, "he, himself."

In more recent times "self" has come to refer to the *core* of one's person, as distinguished from the periphery, so that we say "I was not myself," and we will be understood to be referring to some behavior which we do not wish to "own." Thus we can distinguish between the true self and those aspects of the person which may lie outside the self. This "core" meaning of the self has many of the same characteristics once carried by the term "soul." Hence, self is often used in modern translations of the Bible to express the term *psyche*, formerly translated by "soul." Another meaning is the self which is yet to be actualized in the future, which may not be the same as the present, and less desired, self. This ideal future self may have a very indefinite shape, in contrast to the ideal self at one's core in the present.

For our purposes we need a concept of self that retains its original meaning of both a sameness over time and a sense of ownness. We also need to incorporate some key elements of contributions made by modern psychologies and theologies of the self.

Since William James we have learned to think of the phenomenal self as incorporating both the sense of identity (the "I"), and its extensions—including the body's core and periphery, as well as personal property, such as clothing and cars. From the late psychoanalyst Heinz Kohut, who first developed the notion of self within psychoanalysis (and toward the end of his career, perhaps beyond it), we learned that the self can be understood as incorporating preconscious and unconscious elements associated with the id, superego and unconscious parts of the ego, as well as with the conscious ego. We also learned that the developing self incorporates as "self-objects" those persons to whom it is closely related, and that it has a "bipolar" character of ideals (derived from relationship to mother) and ambitions (derived from relationship to father).[3]

From the Niebuhr brothers, Reinhold, and especially H. Richard, we have learned to think theologically about the self. The former stressed the centering function of the self in his later works. The latter emphasized the relational character of the self, both to other persons and to a "third," who ultimately is God, as well as the unifying function of the self.[4] Thus, the self does provide a connectional concept between theology and psychology, even though it has not been used in precisely the same ways in these disciplines.

The self refers to the felt sense of ownness and sameness that a person perceives, together with their connections below the surface of awareness, and sometimes to disconnected fragments below the surface. This definition emphasizes the so-called subjective self, as opposed to the presumed objective self as perceived by someone else. However, this distinction is not actually clear-cut, since the observer is perceiving what is communicated by the person about that person's self. The observer, if acting capably as a personal counselor or caregiver, may then assist the person to a fuller and more accurate perception of his or her self. That there are psycho-physical structures which underlie awareness and communication may be inferred, and these structures may also be said to be the self. The self is identified in the coherence of awareness of and communication of the sense of ownness and sameness, both over time and of its several aspects in the moment, with the proviso that some aspects may be fragmented and disconnected.

3. *Spirit and Self.* The *interaction* between spirit and self is at the core of the person. Neither can be said to characterize

completely any human action, attitude, thought, or emotional state. Rather, both are involved in some degree, and their interaction gives each person his or her uniqueness. Thus, in any given human behavior either spirit or self may appear to be dominant or decisive, but both are involved. The spirit, in its relational outreach, carries the coloring of the self's identity and self-esteem functions. The idealizing and ambition poles of the self are the vehicles of moral and vocational aspiration of spirit. In moments of passion and confusion the two are mixed, and action is dependent upon intricate intrapsychic balances involving drives, emotions, willing and vision.

In focusing on the interaction of spirit and self I do not intend to neglect the body as the vehicle of interaction. Without proposing a "solution" to the mind-body problem, I affirm the embodiment of both spirit and self with respect to human beings. Without the body the human spirit and self do not exist as human. From a theological perspective the spirit, indeed, we are taught, will return to God upon the death of the body and the self. Nevertheless, as human spirit it requires embodiment. The self permeates the body and is not localized in the brain or nervous system, even though these organs are more central to its functioning than others.

Since this is a book about the pastoral counseling of the aging, I shall try to show how the self-spirit interactional model may especially illumine the lives of older persons, even though I think it applicable to all. So most of the examples in the following discussion of *relational vectors* will be drawn from that group.

4. *Relational Vectors.* Vector is a term in mathematics used to denote direction and magnitude, usually represented by a straight line. In this discussion the term will be used metaphorically to indicate different objects (or subjects) of relationships (direction), and kinds and degrees of attachment (magnitude). This metaphorical use introduces the notion of difference in kind not found in the mathematical term, but it still seems best for my purpose.

I shall call these relational vectors of the spirit to simplify the language and to indicate the leading of the spirit in relationships, although they always involve the self as well. To provide examples we shall sketch seven kinds of human relationships in which older persons are especially likely to be involved: spouses, one's own body, children, friends, the human community, relationships to nature/culture, and divine relationships.

a. *Spousal relationships.* These are likely to be vectors of great magnitude or intensity and complexity, although in some long marriages intensity is reduced, even if complexity is not. The spirits of spouses become intertwined in ways influenced by their self-development, but also modified by their own experience of one another. They do become self-objects to each other to some extent, that is, they incorporate one another into the self system as a part of themselves. Late-life marriages are influenced by previous experience with spouses as well as by the early development of the self. Spirit is involved in all dimensions of marriage, including the ecstatic (out of the self) moments of sexual relations, arguments, companionship, and the minutiae of everyday life.

It is true that it is not common for a wife to say to her husband at the breakfast table, "Your spirit is offending me by its attention to the newspaper." We are accustomed to reserve the term spirit, if we use it at all, for presumably loftier functions. Nevertheless, the ordinary dimensions of life are not really discontinuous from the lofty ones. The husband who is constrained in silence by his wife's repeated insistence that his attire is lacking in neatness and aesthetic appeal may unconsciously find her complaints to remind him of his mother's admonitions, and then reject her as a troublesome self-object by humiliating her in social situations, or by ridiculing her efforts at improving her social station. So also do the spirits of spouses, partially merged through countless small events of mutual gratification, support and uphold one another through major crises.

b. The spirit, influenced by the self, also relates to *one's own body.* In later years this relationship becomes even more important than in earlier life. The maintenance and enhancement of the body's structures and functions need to attain a focal position as a vector of the spirit's relationships as the processes of aging, disease, and accidents begin to manifest themselves. Although the body can become an obsession of the self, in which its every slight alteration becomes a symptom of some dreaded ailment, health is a proper and necessary concern for those who would live their lives fully. Regular exercise and dietary concerns are important components.

We are not accustomed to think of these commonplace concerns about the health of the body in spiritual terms, but it is important to see them as no less spiritual than religious practices, even if we are not into "New Age" cults where they may be blended with reincarnation phenomena. Among the elderly the body is more likely to suffer from neglect than from deliberate mortification, but the results can be equally disastrous.

c. Relating to *one's own children.* This can be a daunting business for the elderly. Although there are many books offering advice to middle-aged children about how to relate to their parents—and these are needed, there is little literature available to help older people with their children. Spirits of older people tend to be intertwined with those of their children only to a slightly less degree than with those of their spouses. Ideally, they would have let their children go to a great extent, and vice versa, but in reality this is seldom the case. Rather, both parents and children remain perhaps overly involved in each other's lives long before infirmity may dictate that children take over the management of the lives of elderly parents.

Most commonly, then, the task of the elderly is a disentangling of spirit from the lives of their children, while maintaining an appropriate affectional relationship. If the self has needs for control over children who are still merged with it as self-objects, this kind of distancing can be a difficult hurdle. Sometimes, too, children are inappropriately attached to, or detached from their elderly parents, provoking distorted relational patterns with the parents. These entanglements of spirit leave both parties often frustrated and angry, with important decisions put into abeyance until a crisis forces an ill conceived one.

d. *Friends.* These are an important relational vector in the lives of the elderly, even more so than in the lives of many younger persons. The spirits of older persons reach out toward friends to compensate for earlier losses of family, especially spouses. Hence, the friendships of the elderly may be more intense than those of their juniors, and subject to the joys and sorrows of such intensity. Many older persons turn their friends into self-objects, thus running the risk of alienation when these friends do not always behave as though they are a part of the self. The loss of friends can also be much more devastating than similar experiences are for those who are younger and who have family and many friends.

In a retirement complex Margaret and Alice became fast friends in a short period of time when they found themselves to be roommates in the intermediate care facility. When Margaret become too infirm to live with the level assistance afforded by the intermediate care facility and had to be moved to the more assisted level in the nursing home, both became ill from the separation, as Alice felt deserted by Margaret at the deeper levels of her self, and Margaret envied Alice her relative independence. Pastoral counseling with the two together could ease the pain of their separation and arrange for them to share time together.

e. *The human community* beyond these primary relationships is also a vector of the human spirit. Even though relationships with the larger community are heavily colored by primary relationships, they have a life of their own in which justice and compassion, as well as, sometimes unfortunately, hatred and fear, play significant roles.

Older people often reduce their investment of spirit in the larger community, but they do not abandon the community altogether. Thoughts and opinions about the sociopolitical scene are often expressed by the elderly in conversation and at the polls—a fact politicians are increasingly appreciating. Some appropriately aspire to leadership positions in their communities for the first time in their so-called retirement years, and successfully carry these out when elected or appointed.

f. Relationships with *nature and culture* are sometimes neglected in the portrayal of the human condition. Although nature and culture are usually separated, and often even regarded as antagonistic, they may be treated together as a vector of the human spirit as the non-human environment which is, indeed, experienced as intertwined, unless one is in a wilderness. Today we have a proper concern for nature which is at special risk from culture. But even this concern is in the service of a more chastened culture intertwined with nature.

Older people may disengage human institutions to some extent, and reengage nature, following Candide's implied advice about cultivating one's garden. Their spirits seek spirit in the aliveness of nature, and in the depths of nature and beyond. Even then nature is discerned with the aid of cultural modes which shape one's vision of nature, even if the vision is of the wilderness to which one repairs to get away from culture. Nevertheless, the longing for nature and life's source through nature is real in the lives of the elderly, who often turn to nature while seeking God.

g. *God.* The human spirit longs for its source, to which it will return, as Augustine said. Thus, *God* is a vector of the human spirit, and at the same time transcends all vectors, as the divine life is present in all the other vectors of spirit which have been briefly discussed above. The presence of God in human relationships is often felt as vocation and the pull or lure toward a future, but also toward family, friends, the human community, and nature/culture. It is also felt in the ideals and in the prohibitions which govern our lives, even though admittedly we often have trouble discerning the ideals and prohibitions which more closely correspond to justice and welfare in the human community as a whole.

For older people, the presence of God as a discrete vector of the spirit is appropriately cultivated along with vocational vision discernable in other vectors. This kind of spirituality, in the more narrow sense of a direct cultivated relationship with God may not characterize all elderly persons, but some further development of interiority is needed to offset physical diminishments which come in some degree to all. Such cultivation of the inner life may take the form of deeper involvement with literature, art, or nature, as well as more traditional forms of the devotional life. But for all, preparation for a return to the source of spirit is needed.

5. *The Quality of Relational Life.* Although it is not necessary to elaborate normative criteria in this chapter that describes the self-spirit model, I shall briefly present some factors which must be considered in making normative judgments

about the quality of relationships and, hence, in this model, of life itself. These factors are strength of spirit, direction of spirit, cohesiveness of self, and availability of relational objects.

a. Strength of spirit, or its intensity. This is closely related to those aspects of personality which are discussed under such topics as ego strength and will, and also to human freedom. It is frequently needed in old age to confront and overcome obstacles which may beset one. Although strength of spirit is dependent upon a degree of physical health, it is not closely correlated with health, and may be expressed through a rather poor physical vehicle.

b. Direction of spirit. Direction of spirit denotes the sum and interplay of relational vectors, so that a sense of vocation can be discerned, as well as the flavor of personality. Not all directions of spirit move the person equally, and they may be in conflict with one another, making overall direction difficult to find, or nonexistent. Nevertheless, direction of spirit, whether detected in many vectors, or noted by its absence, is an important indicator of the quality of relational life. Older persons are at particular risk of lacking direction of spirit, so it is an especially important indicator of quality in their lives.

c. Cohesiveness of self. A term introduced by Kohut, the cohesiveness of the self refers to the relative "sameness" of the developing self in children and young adults, and its relative freedom from hidden fragments. A cohesive self enables one to reach out through spirit in relationships with others, whether human beings, nature, or God, without the need to incorporate them as self-objects, or avoid them by distancing. A self lacking cohesiveness can still be troublesome to older adults, even though they may have coped with their self-fragments for years. For the unpleasant surprises of later years—such as personal losses and attempts to compensate for them which go awry—can retrigger the early buried pain associated with the fragmentation.

d. Availability of appropriate relational objects. That suitable persons and life-giving environmental (nature/culture) relational objects will always be available cannot be taken for granted, especially with reference to older persons, who have some tendency to be isolated. God is always available, but usually cannot be experienced apart from other vectors of the spirit, as noted above.

Availability of appropriate objects can be influenced by the other three factors in the quality of relational life. Cohesiveness of self, together with strength and direction of spirit, can well lead one to seek and find appropriate relational objects. And such relational objects can have a positive reciprocal effect on the other three factors, sharpening vocational vision carried by strength and direction of spirit, and increasing comfort levels in both "ownness" and "sameness" poles of the self.

6. *Conclusion.* In the chapters that follow I shall attempt to show that the self-spirit model of human being is useful and truthful to the best in the Christian tradition and in contemporary thinking about the person in illuminating the issues and processes of pastoral counseling of older people. The basic bipolar model, its relational vectors, and its criteria for quality of relationships will provide a more adequate vehicle than those available for discussing both the heights and the depths of human experience involved in such counseling.

Chapter 5

Pastoral Counseling as Pathway to the Future: An Overview of Its Purpose, Structure, and Processes

1. The *broad purpose* of pastoral counseling with the elderly is to attempt to clarify the future in light of the past and the present, and to find possible pathways to that future. This may seem rather stark in light of the multiple human concerns that may prompt anyone to seek counseling. But the elderly are often especially prone to the sense that they have no future or a very limited one; hence, the importance of establishing the future as a possibility for them. All the multiple concerns hinge on the reality and shape of the future. Without a viable future they tend to dry up.

In this chapter I shall try to show how a sense of the future and a proper attitude toward it can help the spirits of the elderly to reach out toward it, and toward the relational objects involved in the vocational lure of that future. How to achieve this kind of realistic, but potent, vision of the future without abandoning hope on the one hand, or succumbing to a wish-dominated, romantic vision of the future and its pitfalls on the other, has been a theme of many philosophers and theologians since Kierkegaard. These have sometimes been called existentialists, sometimes crisis theologians, and now narrative/hermeneutical thinkers. Charles V. Gerkin's work is a good example of the last named, and will serve us here as a vehicle of discussion.

Gerkin recognizes the models of aging spoken of in chapter 3 as the decremental, and decremental with compensation models, under somewhat different terminology, borrowing the terms symmetrical (decrements of aging seen as the

41

downside of a life cycle curve) and loss/compensation from Paul Pruyser.[1] In addition, Gerkin examines Erikson's epigenetic model which emphasizes integrity vs. despair and finds it helpful in its emphasis on old age as needed for fulfillment of early life trends with integrity. Nevertheless, he proposes his own model—a "historical/eschatological model," to take account of both historical identity and Christian eschatological identity.[2] Gerkin's model is intended to make clear the paradoxical character of aging in that it brings together the elements of the past but also must envision a future which includes dimensions beyond this life to a life with God.

Gerkin's model is only sketched, but it contains the emphasis on the future in tension with (or in paradoxical juxtapostion with) the past and present, which is most pertinent to the lives of the elderly. The general model of human being that is employed in this book, the self-spirit model, requires that the future always be represented as well as the past and present. Whether this emphasis contains an actual logical paradox, as Gerkin suggests, may be questioned, since the reality of God's future may be viewed as encompassing the personal and socio/cultural history of the individual. But for many it does require a stretch beyond ordinary thinking to bring them together, and when this has been done in the past, frequent resort to mind or spirit/body dualism has resulted, as Gerkin suggested. Our embodied self-spirit model rejects this kind of dualism.

For our purpose of finding a suitable way to speak of older people in particular in relation to pastoral counseling, Gerkin's historical/eschatological model has merit, even if its name is a bit awkward. I prefer to downplay the paradox supposedly implicit in the model, and to regard the model as representing potential continuity in our way of thinking about the lives of the elderly, and not radical disjuncture. The paradox results from an assumption of the disjuncture of nature and supernature which is widespread, but not necessarily the most realistic approach. If caregivers can envisage older people as having futures, even if they lie beyond the horizon—futures that involve the past but also transcend the past, and sometimes assist those whom they seek to help to begin to have such a vision, then the model will have done its job.

Within this broad purpose of pastoral counseling as concerned primarily with the future, two kinds of reservations must also be stated. The first is that the focus of counseling is not necessarily always on the future, but is, rather, initially focused where the more immediate concerns of the counselee appear to be, whether past, present or future. Often a concern for losses of various sorts in the present seems to dominate the conversation, but these are seen either explicitly or implicitly against a backdrop of a future which either has meaning or lacks it.

Mrs. B., an 87-year-old Catholic who has recently moved from her long-time residence to live with her daughter and her family, speaks plaintively to Joyce, a caregiver from her church, about her sensory losses, saying that she can no longer see to cook or smell the gas if she fails to light the stove. She notices that she is no longer alert all the time, and finds this frightening, as Joyce empathetically acknowledges. Encouraged by Joyce's support, she speaks of looking forward to going to mass every Sunday, and of her trust in God, to whom she talks a lot about her present circumstances and the future, praying for strength. But also she says sometimes, "Maybe it won't be as long as it might, God?"

The focus here is on present losses made tolerable only by reference to a future with God. She made no reference to life beyond death as such, but her emphasis on positive trusting in the providence of God suggests that this providence will continue after death.

Although this kind of reference to the future is not always specifically present in the verbalizations of pastoral counselees, it is always in the background of conversation that has a constructive thrust. In this instance of pastoral care, the caregiver, Joyce, is sensitive to the plaintive longing expressed by Mrs. B., and also to her seeking God in the mass and in private prayer, and by accepting these expressions enabled her to give voice to her hope of an early death—that is a good death, from her point of view—a death in the arms of God.

The second reservation about the emphasis on the future in pastoral counseling with the elderly concerns the various kinds of problems presented by eschatologies of the past as they have been applied to individuals and interpreted by them. These problems cluster around issues of immortality of the soul in tension with the resurrection of the body, eternal continuity of personal identity in tension with meaningful participation in the life of God, and the problematic of concepts of development applied to soul or spirit after the death of the body— without which no discussion of development seems possible.

Although all of these issues have a reality about them, especially in the eventual logical antimonies and undesirable personal consequences of some modes (of static continuity, for example), for persons seeking to hold the integrity of their lives together by linking their past with a future which has a dimension beyond the grave, they are not of great consequence.

In chapter 4 in the context of the discussion of the spirit and the self, I presented a view of spirit based upon biblical thinking, in which spirit does survive the death of the body, but returns to participate in the life of God, whose special gift it was. This view of a transformed and participatory personal eschatology may not be shared by all the elderly, who often have more individualistic ideas. However, the particularities of personal eschatologies held by the elderly need not overly concern us, unless we think that they are going to prove troublesome to the persons who hold them. Then they need to be challenged.

2. The *structure* of pastoral counseling with elderly individuals may be more flexible than that ordinarily employed by parish ministers. This flexibility applies both to schedule and location, as is noted by Louise O. Bernstein, in discussing secular counseling. Location ". . . might be the client's home, a park bench, or a coffee shop (locations that might seem 'unprofessional' to those not familiar with this type of activity)."[3] Bernstein goes on to say that ". . . because losses, problems, and needs do accelerate with advancing age, it often happens that there cannot be a tidy conclusion to the relationship, which may not actually terminate until the client dies or moves away."[4]

This point will be all the more forceful for ministers in local churches who have, in any case, an ongoing pastoral responsibility. Thus, for parish ministers with limited amounts of time to devote to pastoral care, the time demands of pastoral counseling with the elderly can be daunting, unless careful planning is done to involve both other professionals and trained lay persons in the activity. No more than about four ongoing cases of pastoral counseling should be carried at one time. Also, they should initially plan with their counselees to do not more than about twelve sessions, even though circumstances may dictate more sessions from time to time.

3. The *processes* of pastoral counseling with the elderly involve the counselor in active educating and offering suggestions, more than one might be involved with in counseling with other age groups. Accompanying the counselee on medical visits or visits to possible living facilities is often in order. Such activities are not auxiliary to counseling but are integral to it. The resistance to counseling noted in chapter 2 often means that counseling will begin on a very informal basis and later develop into a more formal relationship, after trust has been established. Often counseling may come about because an elderly caregiver seeks help in the management of a still more elderly parent's situation. In such cases the focus usually quickly shifts to intergenerational and other issues of direct personal concern.[5]

The foregoing paragraph outlines some of the age-specific features of pastoral counseling with the elderly. But there are many features in common with pastoral counseling with other groups. Empathic listening and responding is basic to all forms, and is no less basic to work with the elderly. In the cognitive model to be proposed, interpretation, restructuring of thinking and attitudes, and rehearsals for changing behavior are also needed, as are direct challenges when the trust level is sufficient. More detail regarding counseling models will be presented in chapter 9.

4. *Summary.* An overview of the more practice-oriented second half of this book, including attention to the purpose of pastoral counseling with the elderly, its structure, and its processes, has necessarily been presented here. The broad purpose of pastoral counseling was described as the attempt to clarify the future and its meaning in relation to the past and present. Gerkin's historical/eschatological model of aging, with some modification, was invoked to attempt to clarify this point.

The structure of pastoral counseling was presented as requiring more flexibility of both time and location than most other forms of counseling, although it was recognized that this need for flexibility may be in some tension with the time demands of the parish ministry, thus requiring careful planning.

Processes of pastoral counseling with the elderly include expanded parameters of what may be regarded as counseling, such as active accompaniment to various institutional facilities, and other informal family related activities, as well as educational and informational emphases not always found in counseling. They also include basic procedural elements of all good counseling, such as empathic listening and responding, interpretation, and confrontation when the occasion requires it, as well as some special procedural emphases in a more narrow sense to be presented in chapter 9.

Chapter 6

Indicators for Pastoral Counseling:
Needs and Situations

The needs and situations which may be indicators for pastoral counseling that were sketched in chapter 1 will now be amplified in the light of the theoretical presentations in chapters 2 and 3, and in light of the discussions of models of human beings, and of the elderly in particular, which have been presented in chapters 4 and 5. I hope these discussions will be pointed and detailed enough to assist caregivers in assessing actual situations and personal need, and that they also are clearly linked to foregoing theoretical discussions so that they may be seen as addressing human issues arising in the lives of older people, and not only the particular problems of the aging.

I note here that crises are not treated as such, though pastoral intervention in crises is an oft needed form of pastoral care. Pastoral counseling becomes appropriate after the initial phases of a crisis have been addressed.

1. *Prolonged or Unusual Grief Reactions.* Personal losses at any age tear at the connective relational tissues of spirit and many times they challenge the self in the depths of its identity dimension. But losses late in life are frequently more devastating, as they are often felt to be irreplaceable (even when this is not the reality). Moreover, they are likely to be multiple, with one particular deep loss serving as a trigger of overwhelming grief to which other losses have also been made contributions, as was noted in chapter 3.

Some elderly persons do emerge from even primary losses, such as the loss of a spouse, within a relatively short period of time (a year to two years) with both self and spirit intact and functioning. Increasingly such bereaved persons are making good use of support groups for widows and widowers to work through their grief. But such groups are not for everyone, and even for those who find them helpful, they are not always sufficient. For many, pastoral counseling may be an important element in recovery, or in some cases, the primary vehicle.

Of the kinds of adverse reactions most likely to result in part from unassuaged grief—somatic reactions, severe depression, active alcohol addiction, inappropriate taking of the roles of the deceased, and prolongation of dysfunctional and painful pining—the last named is more likely to be helped by pastoral counseling as a primary mode of assistance, though it may be profitably employed as an adjunct in the others. Colin Murray Parkes in his classic study, *Bereavement,* states that ". . . the pining or yearning that constitutes separation anxiety is the characteristic feature of the pang of grief."[1]

Talking through the pain of separation from a deceased spouse, including both negative and positive feelings, can help a future which appeared cloudy to begin to emerge as a clarified possibility. As bondage to the past is loosened, the future can begin to take on positive meaning. The spirit reaches out, at first perhaps to the counselor, but then, if the counseling is well-done, and the attachment to the counselor understood for what it is, beyond the counselor to others who may be part of the future.

Parkes and others have pointed out that the period of what may be regarded as normal grief for a widow is longer than the traditional one year. Nevertheless, the time does end for normal grief in about two years. If after that time a widow does not resume a more present and future oriented life-style, additional steps, particularly pastoral counseling, ought to be taken.

Widowers are more inclined to somatic reactions and alcohol abuse in bereavement, and may have a difficult time recognizing their problem before it is too late for prevention of serious consequences. But alert pastoral caregivers can nevertheless offer opportunities for counseling which sometimes will be accepted. What is needed is a relationship of accepting and respectful availability to facilitate the move from pastoral care to pastoral counseling.

2. *Depression*. Although depression may occur as a part of, or even as most of, an acute grief reaction, it may also occur independently of any particular immediate loss. Hence, I am presenting it as a separate indicator of need for possible pastoral counseling. It is the single most debilitating ailment afflicting the aging, although it is not confined to older people. I say this, even though there are now some rather solid data challenging the notion that depression is more widespread among the elderly than in younger age groups.[2] Still, for those who have it, and they are many, it is devastating.

Clinical depression is characterized by a sense of burden, or heaviness, low self-esteem, a sense of hopelessness, often by lack of sleep (or too much sleep), lack of appetite, slowness of thought processes, difficulty with decision making, and trouble with normal activity, whether "work" or "play." (That the distinction between work and play is not absolute, and indeed, hardly exists at times, becomes obvious when these ideas are used in a context of official retirement.) It is also often described as very painful, even though specific lesions due to depression are unknown. Depression in the elderly is relatively harder to diagnose than it is in younger persons. It is often confused with a senile dementia, and also often masked by adaptive ego defenses (or formerly adaptive defenses) of denial, counterphobic defenses or somatization.[3]

The proximate cause of depression is increasingly agreed upon as an interruption or diminishment of the flow of information across the synaptic gaps in the brain. Such interruption or diminishment results from the reduction or absence of electrochemical neurotransmitters, most prominently norepinephrine and seratonin. The precise mechanisms involved in these diminishments are still not clearly identified.

Depression is about twice as frequent among women as among men worldwide in industrialized countries.[4] I know of no evidence that suggests that this ratio does not hold up for the older segment of the population.

Though the underlying causes of depression which produce the depletions in neurotransmitters are still being clarified, for a long time some distinction has been made between reactive or situational depression, and endogenous (coming from within) depression, and this distinction still seems to have merit, even though both genetic and environmental factors often seem to play a part. In elderly populations loss of close personal relationships and loss of a sense of being in control of one's own life, sometimes called ego or self-loss, are most frequently predominant factors.

Bipolar illness, in which depression may be a major symptom (the opposite pole of manic, or hypomanic, excitement), is more certainly caused by hereditary factors. Bipolar illness seems to be found less frequently among the elderly than are the depressive reactions as such.

What can pastoral counseling, in either individual or group mode, contribute to the alleviation of depression, a human condition that is thought to have a physiological deficit as a central component of its configuration? Antidepressant drugs and electroconvulsive therapy have both been used to treat depression successfully, but the former, especially, has often been used in combination with psychotherapy. Weinstein and Khanna cite several studies of group therapy with elderly persons who had, among others, depressive symptoms, and which had positive outcomes.[5] They also cite similar effects of individual treatment in cases with similar mixed symptomatic pictures.[6]

In my view pastoral counseling can serve as a valuable modality in combating depression if it can be started early in the process when the depression is relatively mild. Persons at this stage feel sad or down, but their feelings fluctuate during the day. They may have sleeping and appetite problems, and wake early. If the reaction has become acute, pastoral counseling may be an accompaniment or follow-up to treatment with drugs or electroconvulsive therapy. Here the close analogy to supportive psychotherapy, thought to be necessary as an accompaniment to antidepressant drugs by many researchers and clinicians, is quite clear.[7]

Pastoral counseling can bring the "there and then" factors, such as relational or self-losses, which contributed to the development of the depression, into focus with the possibilities held by the future in the light of personal and theological resources. It can assist the elderly person to regain his or her footing which has been lost amid shifting sands of the outer and inner environment of aging, and to begin to walk in a chosen direction.

Hammer cites a case of a 68-year-old-man who was a professional pianist, who became depressed when the onset of arthritis and failing eyesight prevented him from continuing his profession, and he had also lost his spouse. Future oriented brief psychotherapy, in which the therapist actively participated with the client in finding a new vocational focus in teaching piano, enabled him to give up ruminations about personal injustice, the death of his wife, and expression of the fear of death to focus instead on his new occupation. After six sessions he terminated treatment, feeling that he no longer needed it.[8] Similar results could have been obtained through pastoral counseling, although the emphasis on the future in pastoral counseling would have perhaps engaged him longer.

Depression is a shutting down, or near shutting down, of the human self-spirit system. In depression the spirit wilts and no longer reaches out to others, vocation, and God. In this sense it is the spiritual malaise *par excellence*. It is appropriate that pastoral counseling, the helping modality with spirit most clearly in focus, be among those most clearly useful in combating it.

3. *Self-Identified Focal Spiritual Questions.* These are questions and anxieties identified by the person who has them as being in some central way "spiritual." In this book the terms spirit and spiritual have been given very broad significance in human life. But it must be recognized that many persons will continue to view a much narrower range of issues and questions as being "spiritual" in character. It is to these questions that I am referring in this section.

The great trans-cultural questions such as the fears of death and dying and how to cope with them, how to have a right relationship with divine life, and how to maximize one's own development in the service of such a relationship are among the self-identified focal spiritual questions. So are those related to right thinking and acting in particular faith traditions. All these questions inevitably involve the self as well as the spirit, so in that sense are no more spiritual than many other questions, such as those involved in producing depression, which was discussed in the previous section. Nevertheless, we need to focus upon them as clear indications of pastoral need and often for pastoral counseling.

Not everyone fears death very much. (Although many of us fear a painful and degrading dying process—which becomes a concern of pastoral counseling when it is imminent or when preventive measures are being pondered.) Yet the fear of death as such did become a significant part of the anxiety picture in the lives of 26 percent of one sample of Americans living in small towns, who also felt that their lives were a failure.[9] Clearly, the fear of death is linked to the loss of hope of renewal when no renewal is thought possible. It is a part of an affective/cognitive syndrome of hopelessness, a true malaise of the spirit which can be addressed, though sometimes with difficulty, by pastoral counseling.

Felt deficits or distortions in one's relationship to God may, to be sure, be addressed in significant ways through education and spiritual direction or guidance. But pastoral counseling may also be very useful in dealing with those aspects of the relationship which impinge most directly upon the self and its close connection to spirit. Much the same can be said about questions of spiritual development. Pastoral counseling may helpfully address aspects of questions related to spiritual development, even though spiritual direction may be needed as well. In my view both counseling and direction may well be done by one person, if that person has the flexibility and training necessary.

Having said this, I must also say that not many elderly people present as focal problems their relationship to God and their spiritual development. We know that this generation of the elderly are more religious by most measures than are younger persons.[10] Most carry into their latter years the same sense of a relationship to God and their own spiritual development which they had in middle life, and do not find either to be a problem, as such, even though they may have complaints in their religious life and we might think their relationship to God less than satisfying. They may, indeed, have needs in these areas which may be touched by addressing other problems they feel that they face, especially in the vectors of interpersonal relationships. A vexed relationship with an aged parent, for instance, may interfere with a more helpful and satisfying relationship with God. If the relationship with the parent is dealt with helpfully, the relationship to God may be positively affected, especially if it then receives some proper attention.

Spiritual problems focused on doctrine and practice of particular faith groups are best dealt with by educational approaches. However, the personal and interpersonal dimensions involving self-spirit relationships may often helpfully be addressed by pastoral counseling.

4. *Problems with Children.* We are more accustomed to think of this area in terms of problems that middle-aged caregivers have with their elderly parents. The middle-aged may, indeed, need help, but they are not the focus of our study. Older people are frequently perplexed about their relationships with their children—how much to rely on them, how much to trust them, sometimes how to get away from them. Often, these conflicts revive earlier scenarios that the elderly had with their children, or even relational patterns that they had with their own parents. Both such patterns are "unfinished business," and as such tend to create some static in the current communication system between the elderly and their children.

The stories which are often repeated, especially by persons in their 80s and 90s, about events which took place much earlier in their lives, frequently touch on such unfinished business. Thus, these audiotape-like repeated stories both reveal and conceal events of great personal importance; they are never mere "idle" reminiscence. As indicated above, they are mostly likely to be of importance in their relationships with their children, although they may have a role to play in other areas of concern; for example, in a relationship with a dead or living spouse.

Probing the meaning of these "tapes" is sometimes a delicate matter, and should be undertaken with caution. Nevertheless, it may be very worthwhile as a means of enhancing current relationships and of providing more integrity to the self-spirit by releasing it from the conflicts of the past.

All troubled relationships with children do not require the

unraveling of old memory tapes. But many do require pastoral assistance of a flexible kind, which may well include some focused pastoral counseling about current relationships with the elderly parent. Sometimes, of course, family pastoral counseling may be in order as well, if the children are available.

5. *Interpersonal and Institutional Rejection.* This area of concern can be a problem, especially for older persons living alone, of whom there are, of course, many. When key persons or institutions, through their representatives, personally reject an older person, the effect on the life of that person can be devastating. Even though such rejection is not usually intended, rejection is often felt when personal investment or integrity is at stake. The rejecting persons are usually those who are felt to be close friends, and institutions are of primary importance—such as churches or in some instances, social clubs or political organizations.

It is true that such experiences can come to anyone at any time of life. But the elderly are often more vulnerable, because there are fewer available compensatory vectors of spirit, and because these experiences frequently come on top of keenly felt losses.

It takes a sensitive pastoral caregiver to detect and respond to a sense of rejection engendered by the church that he or she may be serving, or more commonly, by one of the organizations within the church. Clues that may indicate personal rejection are, for instance, complaints about structural aspects of organizations, such as a singles club, which shield individuals from blame, but which nevertheless point to defects in the system.

6. *Vocational Questions.* If the reader has been following the general line of thinking in this book, it will not be surprising that vocational questions are among the major concerns said to be possibly helped by pastoral counseling. Nevertheless, it is worth noting that vocation is not a usual topic in books about older people, who are usually thought to be too old for vocational pursuits, and that avocations and hobbies are the most that can legitimately be said to be appropriate for them. That is, they are felt to be capable of auxiliary activities, but not principal activities. When the matter is put this way we can see that

this seems to be a rather absurd way to look at it—and indeed it is!

Vocation is literally a call into a future, and many older persons experience such calls. In some way all do, as all look to a future, although the voice of the call may be very faint. But for many in their 60s and 70s the call is heard as being loud and clear, even though the culture may not provide opportunities to heed it. The call may not be for gainful employment, though not infrequently older people feel that they have to be paid for what they do, or it is not really a vocation—a troublesome factor in a world reluctant, in spite of recent national legislation to prevent involuntary retirement, to employ older people. Thus, the need for pastoral counseling often arises to help the person to clarify what a reasonable vocational goal may be, and to help deal with the frustrations which may arise in the attempt to actualize it.

Vocation, by theological definition, is always ultimately the call of God, but usually it is mediated by many other vectors of the spirit, including the interpersonal vectors which often provide a sense of need, and the nature/culture vector, which provides the sense of structured opportunity. All of these vectors may need attention in pastoral counseling focused on vocational issues.

Vocation is in some way always central to one's felt identity at the heart of the self-system, and hence is never a minor matter for older persons, as it also is not for others. Their complex motivations surrounding the vocational lure of the future require as much attention as do those of younger persons. A woman in her 70s who became a social worker relatively late in life found herself restless in retirement, after having worked most of her career as a hospital social worker assisting persons in post-hospitalization rehabilitation. She tried repeatedly to secure part-time employment as a social worker, but was not successful. She found partial satisfaction through various volunteer activities in church and community, but her background had instilled into her the need for gainful employment to be a fully identified human being. Although well-meaning friends and some counselors advised her to accept retirement, she persisted until she found an agency willing to employ her part-time. Even though the work was not that for which she was very well-suited and the pay was low, she became very much more contented with her life and its sense of vocation fulfillment.

Both Eugene C. Bianchi and David Gutmann, in rather different studies, have stressed the marked need in our society to view the post-60 years as a time of active contribution to society. Says Bianchi, in his study of aging as a spiritual journey, "Throughout the chapters on midlife and elderhood we also emphasized the double and interlinking of the need for a contemplative middle age and an old age turned back toward the service of the world."[11] Gutmann, in *Reclaimed Powers: Toward a New Psychology of Men and Women in Later Life*, a study of aging in four cultures, puts forward the thesis that evolutionary design of cultures requires that elders offer creative guidance to their cultures. "The same evolutionary design that has made the presence of elders a permanent feature of our species is recapitulated in individual lives, as aging men and women develop new, hitherto-unclaimed capacities that enlarge their lives and that fit them for their special social and species assignments."[12]

Without necessarily endorsing all aspects of the thinking of these two scholars, I believe that they make important points, and that we must work toward making our society more receptive to the contributions that can be made by older persons. Without this kind of cultural change, the pastoral counseling of older people in the vocational area will become increasingly frustrating for both counselor and counselee.

7. *Marriage Counseling.* Marital problems are what most often prompt the elderly to seek counseling. Stresses in this area are sometimes so acute that they lead older people to take the initiative in seeking help more often than distress in other dimensions of their lives. Marriage is the major source of personal support for many of the elderly, whether it be a marriage of long duration or one recently entered into after the loss of an earlier spouse, or a first marriage. This support function, as well as other complicating emotional components which form a part of most marriages, bring the elderly to overcome their resistance to "mental" kinds of helping and to seek counseling.

This initiative (which, to be sure, is not always present in cases of need for marriage counseling among the elderly) is both a blessing and a potential curse for those engaging in marriage counseling with older persons. The problem is that some such persons who come for help are not prepared to engage in reflective exploration of the situation according to any contemporary model of counseling. Rather, their personal development took place in the pre-mental health era. They seek authoritative answers to their dilemmas and firm directions about how to proceed. It may well be that the younger persons in the current generation of the elderly are more amenable as a group to modern reflective methods, but many still are not readily able to engage in such counseling. Hence, would-be pastoral marriage counselors working with the elderly need to be flexible in their approach, lest they lose those who come to them for help.

The goals of marriage counseling with the elderly do not differ markedly from those which are appropriate for younger persons, even though the methods sometimes do. The general goal of marriage counseling should always be to promote the best personal interests of both parties, whether this be the strengthening and continuation of the marriage, or in cases where the marriage is not viable, the enabling of the two parties to end it while still in communication with one another. With older persons, perhaps a tilt toward the preservation of the marriage—a little beyond the tilt that ministers are inclined to have with any couple, may be in order, since the opportunities for remarriage may be rather limited. On the other hand, marriages involving older persons should not be held together for the sake of the marriage any more than other marriages.

8. *Other Indicators.* Other possible indicators for pastoral counseling include, especially, changing locations and issues arising in efforts to care for still more elderly parents, as well as other crises requiring decisions which are brought on by changing circumstances or health status.

Older people facing possible changes in their living arrangements do most often arrive at their decisions without any kind of professional help. However, when a pastoral caregiver knows that an elder is facing such a decision, it is a good idea to be particularly available to him or her, for such decisions are best made in some kind of consultation, even though this may not be formal counseling in any sense.

Increasingly, older persons face decisions regarding the care of their still older parents, and often can use the help of a caregiver in making these. Occasionally, formal counseling is indicated because of the long-term relationships involved which make constructive decision making difficult without some attention to the interpersonal histories—attention which can best be effected through pastoral counseling. Such counseling can attend the wounds to self and spirit which may be preventing decisions for the best care arrangements from being made.

9. *Conclusions.* Any of the numerous crises that arise in the lives of most elderly persons, whether due to external circumstances or to illness, may be occasions for pastoral counseling, although they are not necessarily such occasions. Among factors of importance in making the determination about the appropriateness of counseling are readiness for counseling and ability to engage in it, the degree to which the matter is impacted by past relationships which could be explored and perhaps loosened in counseling, and availability of time and suitable environment. In many instances, responsive pastoral care may be all that is necessary, or that the circumstances allow.

Chapter 7

The Contexts of the Pastoral Counseling of the Elderly

In 1961 Seward Hiltner and Lowell G. Colston published a volume entitled *The Context of Pastoral Counseling*. In this book Hiltner and Colston showed that the context in which counseling is done makes a considerable difference in who comes for counseling and in outcome. This study, which was a comparison of counseling done by the same person (Colston) in a church and in a university counseling center, defined context as having four dimensions: Setting, Expectation, Shift in Relationship, and Aims and Limitations.[1] The specific findings of this study do not concern us here, but the general finding that the context of pastoral counseling can significantly affect the counseling process does concern us.

For our purposes the first two dimensions of context are of great importance, and the last two of lesser importance, but still of some significance. *Setting* and *expectation* are the crucial variables in the three contexts which will be in focus in this volume: the age-integrated, or "normal" community; a large, age-segregated retirement community in which the majority of persons are homeowners, and a smaller, living arrangement stratified, continuing-care retirement community, or, "life-care facility," as such institutions are sometimes called. *Shift in relationship* does not always apply in these settings, since pastoral counseling may or may not be done by the pastor of the church to which the person belongs. *Aims and limitations* may be affected by context, and some attention will be given to this point, even though it is not a major focus of the present study.

1. *Age-Integrated Communities.* There are, of course, a great variety of these. Virtually all communities in the United

States have some proportion of older people. Since these are composed of differing social classes, ethnic groups, and types of community (urban, suburban, small town, rural), the contexts in which most older people live in the United States exert widely differing influences upon them.

In a recent AARP survey of Americans over 55 years of age, 86 percent said that they wished to remain in their homes after retirement.[2] This figure seems congruent with earlier surveys which indicated that only about 12 percent of Americans move anywhere at or after retirement, including 5 percent who eventually move to nursing homes (up from 2.5 percent in the 1960s).[3] Thus, the vast majority at the present time remain at home, wherever that may be.

In 1989 I was afforded a small window on this vast population through the Suzanne Paterson Center of Princeton, NJ. I became acquainted with several visitors to this center for the elderly and the handicapped through playing chess and bridge and through conversation. In these conversations the issue of pastoral counseling was not directly in view, with one exception.

Upon learning of my interest in the pastoral counseling of the elderly, Mrs. Thomas, an elderly woman, told me of a recent extremely unpleasant encounter with a young man who had insulted and assaulted her in the course of a matter involving a possible fender bender. She had not pressed charges against him, for fear that he might try to take vengeance on her. She said that she, and other senior citizens, did not need counseling, as they could take care of themselves. But young people did need it, as evidenced by the young man. She then became tearful as she told me of her loss of her son, a physician, to cancer four years previously, and her feeling of the injustice of this loss when juxtaposed to the life of the young man who had insulted and assaulted her.

I believe that her attitude of determined independence, which existed side by side with psychic wounds resulting from loss, and for which I thought she could use some pastoral care, if not pastoral counseling, would not be atypical of those older persons whom I knew at the Suzanne Paterson Center, although I could not claim that it characterized each and every one. They presented a cheerful countenance to the world, even though several had had major losses due to health problems and bereavement. My opinion is that this was due more to their personality characteristics than to any particular effect of their community setting in a rather bustling university town, although such an effect cannot be ruled out. Since mental health facilities were readily available in the community and their use rather encouraged by the cultural climate, a specific dampening effect on readiness for pastoral counseling cannot be assumed, unless it also be assumed that these senior citizens dichotomized pastoral counseling as something to be avoided from other forms of personal helping—an unlikely assumption.

The United States as a whole is probably not as encouraging as the atmosphere in Princeton to those who might be in need of personal help, although we must again recall how difficult cultural generalizations are. Even allowing for this difficulty, the modal atmosphere in which most older persons live does not encourage them to seek personal help. As we noted in chapter 2, they are still regarded as not quite human or worth troubling with by many helping professionals, including many of the clergy, even though this attitude is hopefully changing. This communication from the culture which includes specifically the churches, coupled with their own fear of being found to be mentally ill, tends to keep the elderly from seeking appropriate pastoral counseling and other forms of mental/spiritual help.

This is so, even though a recent study by Peter Lewinsohn and his colleagues has called into question a presumed lack of self-esteem among the elderly, another factor in their failure to seek help appropriately. In this study ". . . older people not only reported being less depressed, but also said they were as active, as involved and less stressed than younger people."[4] Older people, perhaps necessarily for some, do engage in a certain amount of denial of difficulty, as was suggested in the anecdote about Mrs. Thomas, and it may have been that this study reflected some of that.

Overall, my best judgment about the contexts of age-integrated communities is that they are neutral to mildly negative in their influence on the pastoral counseling of the elderly.

A pervasive atmosphere of denial is not present for them, since they are defined as out of the mainstream. But neither are they encouraged to seek help. Often they feel that a stiff upper lip is the best countenance to turn to the world.

2. *Age-Segregated Retirement Communities: Homeowner Mode.* Since the 1950s this type of community has been growing in size and numbers in the United States, especially in Arizona, California, and Florida. The largest of these communities is comprised of Sun City, Arizona and its newer contiguous companion, Sun City West. Sun City was founded in 1960 by the Del Webb Development Corporation, and Sun City West about 20 years later by the same organization. Together they have a population of about 65,000 which is restricted, with certain exceptions, to persons over 55 years of age. A slightly older and much smaller community of about 2500, Youngtown, also contiguous with Sun City, is comprised mostly of older people, although is not now restricted to them. Sun City has become a model for 85 communities across the country.[5]

In the AARP survey mentioned earlier in this chapter, only 12 percent of respondents indicated that they would like to live in an age-segregated community (about 5 percent actually do), and fewer still seemed ready to move far from their homes to achieve this. Furthermore, living in such communities flies in the face of both conventional and expert opinion, which holds that older people are better off in age-integrated communities where they can affect, and be affected by, persons in other age groups.

However, these communities have a special interest for our concerns in this book, I believe, for two reasons. The first is, that given the ever-increasing numbers of the elderly in our society, larger numbers of them, and probably larger percentages of them (pending, however, a favorable economic climate during the next decade) will be living in age-segregated communities of the homeowner type. (I note here that not everyone in Sun City, Arizona, is a homeowner, but homeowning is the predominant mode of residence.) These communities came into being during a time of relative affluence and increasing health resources which made them possible. Even modicums of these elements will probably continue to fuel the Sun Cities and the sense of independence which they foster.

The second reason these communities are of interest in this study is that they represent the kind of community ethos which older people themselves create, in the sense that they took what the developer gave them and maintained, developed, and expanded it. At least it is the kind that the current cohorts of middle and upper middle-class Americans create. Thus, they may provide clues for the influence of the thinking and attitudes of the elderly which affect pastoral counseling done even in other settings. During the winter of 1990 I spent two months in Sun City, Arizona, trying to understand it better.

a. The Sun Cities—some general characteristics. Frances Fitzgerald, writing primarily about Sun City Center, Florida, founded by Del Webb at about the same time as Sun City, Arizona, made these comments about this kind of retirement community:

> Even those gerontologists who have registered objections to Rose's thesis (that there is a national subculture of the aging) would admit that in certain communities retired people are inventing new kinds of relationships, new ways of spending their time, and new ways of dealing with death. The Sun Cities and Leisure Worlds are without precedent; no society recorded in history has ever had whole villages—whole cities—composed exclusively of elderly people.[6]

These are, indeed, pioneers in a new life-style of aging, as Fitzgerald has said elsewhere. She also said they are not Puritans in the sense that they felt their work to be socially necessary, a point with which I agree.[7]

But the Sun Cities are a kind of last outpost of Calvinism in the sense of the cultural manifestation of the impact of Reformed theology and practice. This kind of culture-Calvinism can characterize persons of varied backgrounds, many of whom had no direct contact with any of the branches of the Reformed ecclesiastical tradition, such as Presbyterianism or the United

Church of Christ. Sun Citians are fiercely independent, believe in the necessity of hard work, even though most no longer practice it, and that they have earned leisure. They tend to be among the more affluent of the relatively wealthy (relative to former times, prior to 1960) elderly in the United States, and pay a lot of real estate and income taxes to the state of Arizona, but have repeatedly voted down school bond issues—a fact that propels many residents into volunteer activities in nearby school districts, and to give cash donations to them. They play a lot of golf (Sun City, Arizona has 18 courses, public and private) and considerable bridge, both of which are, or may be, highly competitive, and also clearly defined by rules. They also volunteer in very large numbers for all kinds of community related activities, including hospital and church related work, but also many other varieties. I attended a celebration of volunteers held as a part of the 30th-anniversary observance in Sun City, Arizona, at which about 2000 persons were present. They tend to be joiners of community organizations, including the Republican Party, but not too active in these organizations. Compared with the population of the U.S. of comparable age, persons 77 to 81 years old in Sun City were twice as likely to be childless (19 percent and 36 percent respectively).[8] They tend to be boosters of Sun City and to give positive responses to "life satisfaction" questionnaires to a greater degree than retired persons in the midwest or in age-integrated communities in the southwest.[9]

Whether childless or not, Sun Citians are likely to be, or at least hope to be, independent of their children, and to have children who are relatively independent of them. Among the men military officers, engineers, corporate middle managers, school administrators, and small-business men predominate. Among the women, a large number of nurses and teachers are to be found (which is not surprising, since these were the principal professions open to women of this generation).[10] It is important to them to be, and to be perceived as independent, active, and happy.

Unlike most older Americans, who tend to be personally religious but do not attend church very often, Sun Citians who belong to churches, about 50 percent of them, attend in large numbers. I estimated that in the winter months when I was there, between 75 and 80 percent of the members of churches in the predominantly Protestant community were in attendance on a given Sunday, plus visitors. This compares with nationwide attendance percentages probably in the 30s.

One of the most prominent attributes of the Sun Cities, noticed immediately by virtually everyone who visits them, is their neatness—some would say excessive neatness. In Sun City, Arizona, row upon row of decorative orange trees line the streets. Any leaves or fruit that drop are immediately picked up and disposed of, as is any other object in any yard which might be construed as detritus. Not to dispose of these stray objects immediately is to invite a phone call from a neighbor suggesting that this be done. Interiors are much the same, except that they do express the occupants' taste and individuality in the art objects which are ensconced amid the tidiness.

This characteristic is of some importance in this study. For one thing, it shows the investment that the communities have in neatness as such. But it also shows that, in keeping with continuity theory, neatness characterized these older persons long before they came to the Sun Cities. People do not learn the habits needed for neatness at retirement age. Or to put the matter in broader perspective, Sun Citians were culture-Calvinists in their former communities, in all probability rather restless with their lack of neatness, among other failings. Cleanliness is, after all, next to, if not identical with, godliness.

A characterological corollary to this neatness is a high degree of rectitude in business and personal life. A real estate agent with whom I had some dealings told me that Sun Citians, and would-be Sun Citians, always keep their word, which makes the area a much more pleasant place to do business than others he had been in previously.

Fitzgerald believes that a new attitude toward death may be evolving in the age-segregated retirement communities like the Sun Cities. This new attitude is characterized by tacit, and more or less silent, acceptance of death as a regular occurrence in community life. Disposal of remains is increasingly by cremation, partly on economic grounds, but made possible by a rather liberal, or at least non-literal, theology.[11] I tend to concur, although I found a good deal of denial, as well.

Somewhat paradoxically, at least on the surface, the propensity of many Arizona Sun Citians to visit regularly the gambling casinos in Laughlin, Nevada, also seems to me to be a late expression of culture-Calvinism. More than one told me that many felt that they had worked hard all their lives and now they were entitled to a little fun.

I myself made an overnight visit to Laughlin, a strip of asphalt in the desert paralleling the Colorado River across from Bullhead City, Arizona. There are eleven casinos, seven with hotels attached, on the strip. Together with a couple of gas stations and a few residences, they comprise Laughlin. There is no mayor, no hospital, and no police force. The people who service the patrons at the casinos live, for the most part, in Bullhead City, which is itself a boom town making very heavy demands on the school system of rural Mohave County, Arizona. In short, Laughlin is a "no frills" Las Vegas. There are no elaborate floor shows; hotel lobbies are totally dedicated to gambling and the uproar accompanying it. Cocktail waitresses bring coffee or liquor to the slot and video poker players at 7:30 AM. Since many of the guests are retirees who tend to be regular in their habits, there are generally more persons eating breakfast in the casinos of Laughlin than, I believe, is true in other casinos.

Not all the gamblers come from Sun City, of course, though busloads do arrive several times a week. Many come from other retirement communities and trailer parks throughout the California, Nevada, Arizona border region and beyond. One gambler from Montana, after losing, by his account, $3000 at a $1 poker video machine, expressed his attraction to this rather stark, gaudy, and noisy environment this way. "You can smell money here. It has sound. It has taste. It's a whole new sensation. And I like it."[12] Perhaps he spoke for many, even though there may be basic differences between his stated sensory motivation and those of the Sun Citians who seem to be relaxing well-crafted controls of life, limb, and money through the medium of specie "play." This kind of "letting go" is still done by the rules, of course. And winning is not out of the question, although it does not seem to be mainly in view, either.

b. The Arizona Sun Cities—some individual citizens. In order to put some flesh on these bones of personality and community characteristics, and to show that individuals transcend them in some respects, I am going to present briefly three profiles of persons, two men and one woman, on the basis of interviews with them.

Tom, age 86, was living in the independent section of a multilevel life-care community near Sun City at the time I met him. He had been a resident of the Sun Cities for 15 years prior to his moving into the life-care community a short time before. Before moving to Sun City he ran a small business in an academic community in Wisconsin. He and his wife visited Sun City several times before making a decision to come. "We had come out for vacations and I enjoyed it and so did she and I just figured I wanted to start, I wanted to get new territory." Unhappily, Tom's wife died of cancer before they could come, but he came alone, anyway.

In his statement about "starting" and "new territory," Tom sounded one of the very modal notes of Sun City life, and one that Frances Fitzgerald identified as the American pioneer spirit of radical change at work in these retirement communities.[13] This generation of older people is the first to live on the frontier of old age as an intact entity.

After arriving in Sun City in bereavement, Tom nevertheless started a new occupation at age 70. After two years he became a real estate agent, learning the occupation and the laws of Arizona which pertained to it, and practiced for about nine years, before retiring for a second time.

Like 95 percent of Sun Citians, Tom opposed incorporation—both Sun Cities in Arizona remain unincorporated. Although he did not state his reason in so many words, he did say that "the more government you get . . . " with the implication that more government means loss of independence, and might threaten the age restriction policy on homeownership (age 55). He did indicate that it would come eventually, he thought, after more of the original homes have been resold.

Tom is now in failing health, but until recently he was a member of the Sheriff's Posse in Sun City, the volunteer law enforcement body—and the only law enforcement body in Sun City on a regular basis. Said Tom about this post-80 phase of his career: "We did a good patrol. They knew we were here."

He has attended no church in Sun City regularly, but considers himself to be a practicing Christian. He retains membership in a fundamental Baptist congregation in Wisconsin, and likes to watch Jerry Falwell on TV.

Tom is a kind of outsized paradigm of one kind of Sun City character—the lonely pioneer who, despite the loss of his spouse, makes a successful second career in real estate after age 70, and makes a final vocational move to Sheriff's Posse before being stopped by health problems. At the time of this interview he still had a dry sense of humor and a twinkle in his eye—a true American classic who made a late move to the frontier.

The second Sun Citian to be here profiled briefly is R. B. (Bruce) Norris (his actual name), who was at the time the president of the Sun City Recreation Board, the most powerful and prestigious post in Sun City (recall that there is no official government in this community of 46,000, since it is unincorporated). Mr. Norris is a retired engineer, formerly employed by a multinational construction concern, and about 72 years of age at the time of the interview. He lives with his wife of many years in a free-standing home on a quiet street in Sun City's middle (in terms of chronology of development) phase. They have three sons who live and work in distant places. Mr. Norris loves to play golf, even though he acknowledges that it has little value as exercise. The Norrises are not currently affiliated with any church.

Part of the interview was focused upon Mr. Norris' concerns with the Recreation Board. Responding to my comment that he had risen quickly to a position of leadership after only one year on the Board, he said in part:

Well, we have had so many problems in the community in the last few years that I think we finally have a good hard-working group of people on the Board—people who want to accomplish certain specific things while they are in office, and they decided that I could very well direct the activities because they knew where my priorities were. . . . I consider myself not the President of the Board, but one of the Directors. . . .

In response to a query about what goals he has for the Board, he continued:

Well, we have a number of priorities. But first we want to have greater participation by our membership in all the various facilities we have. I think that is the most important thing that we can do. We want to achieve a relationship with Sun City West which will allow us a greater interchange between the two groups . . . .

These excerpts give us some flavor of Mr. Norris' view of himself as a *primus inter pares* on the Recreation Board. He went on to describe his efforts to respond personally to complaints that citizens made about actions taken by one or another of the ten Recreation Centers, attempting to improve a rather poor public relations posture and to offer a more sympathetic approach to problems frequently brought on by illness.

In response to my inquiry about his perception of the need for personal counseling in the community, he said, "I think that rec centers not only provide an outlet for exercise, but they provide an outlet for mental stimulation which is for me as important as anything you can have." In this connection it came to light in the interview that Mr. Norris considered himself to be a kind of counselor to people who have worked for him over the years. He told one story about a glum associate with whom he worked years ago, and who he got to smile and speak to him on the job. "I've always had people working for me and if you are going to get the best out of people, they have to have the right mental attitude."

Bruce Norris is a tough minded engineer "with a heart of gold," and also with some leadership ability that he is now happily using, hopefully to benefit his community. There are many men of similar character in the Sun Cities, though not all have his ability.

The third and last citizen about whom a sketch is presented is Grace, the volunteer. As noted earlier, there are many volunteers in these communities in which volunteerism is central to the way of life. But Grace nevertheless stood out. At the time I interviewed her she was still recovering from a serious heart attack about five months previously, and was trying to sell her home and move to one of the life-care facilities in the area. She had been widowed a year and a half before.

Grace had a history of volunteering even before moving to Sun City from the east coast, particularly in church related activities. She served as a high ranking lay officer in her church in the 1960s, when it was uncommon for women to do so. Since coming to Sun City she again served as a church officer, and also as a volunteer in a local arts group, where she did publicity, in the local hospital, with her husband, at Recording for the Blind, also with her husband, and at the library. She did not seem to think all this volunteer activity was in any way extraordinary, recounting it by searching her memory in run-on fashion; "And then I volunteered at the library. I worked there for many years and I had cancer and I gave that up, and let's see what else did we do." On the question of whether there might be needs of a personal nature unmet by present community services which might be met by pastoral counseling, Grace said she ". . . did not know of any people who have had a great occasion to call upon it." She also felt her own bereavement had been well taken care of by the ministers and laity of the large mainline Protestant church in which she has been an officer. She was quite apologetic about her lack of information on the topic of unmet needs, in keeping with her marked characterological bent to be helpful.

In her life before Sun City Grace had been a secretary, albeit a rather powerful one. But clearly her vocation has long been expressed through what is called volunteerism, and only expanded in vectors of helpfulness after arrival in Sun City. Her bereavement has been a hard one, but her spirit still reaches out.

c. The Sun Cities—implications for pastoral counseling. Anyone seeking to make a case for the need for pastoral counseling in places like Sun City would seem, at first glance, to have a very tall order on his or her hands. Rather, on the surface the principal implication about pastoral counseling seems to be that pastors elsewhere should counsel their parishioners to leave and go to Sun City. My interviewees did not acknowledge any personal need for such a thing, or any knowledge of it going on in the community. Interviews with several ministers in the Sun Cities and one director of an interfaith counseling service in Phoenix, generally confirmed this lack of pastoral counseling in the area, and skepticism on the part of some that it was needed. The director and his group did a limited amount of marriage counseling with the elderly in the area, and one minister with whom I talked did some very short-term counseling with a few of his parishioners.

Attempts to measure life satisfaction, or in plain English, happiness, as we have noted, have almost uniformly resulted in high marks for the age-segregated, homeowner communities. Activity and optimism are more than slogans, they are *de rigueur*. Perhaps the most blatant manifestation of this spirit, and perhaps an over-expression of it, is in the Sun Cities Poms, a group of women cheerleaders between the ages of 63 and 85 who perform at athletic and other community functions, and who are looked upon askance by some Sun Citians. On the note that the Poms might represent some kind of over-protestation, I turn to a psycho-social analysis of Sun City attitudes which may have a bearing on the pastoral counseling question.

It was noted earlier that Sun Citians have responded more positively on life satisfaction surveys than have older persons in age-integrated communities in the midwest and southwest. Bultena and Wood, whose work was cited, makes several useful points about this finding. In the first place, Sun Citians have a higher educational level, economic level, and perceived health level than do the other groups, so that the specific role of the environment may be questioned.[14] This finding raised, once again, questions about the significance of environment in the lives of older people, an unresolved matter. On the other hand, the environment did provide relative freedom from the stress caused by an emphasis on instrumental and productive values, and it provided individuals with more opportunities for friendship into advanced years.[15]

More recently some researchers have raised questions about the global character of the concepts employed in the life satisfaction, morale, and adjustment surveys. Larson found several dimensions but thought they were highly correlated and pointed to an underlying "subjective well-being" factor.[16] However, Cutler found Larson's conclusion to be simplistic, since the scales measure different phenomena in different age groups, and often share items which produce intercorrelations.[17]

Although it is not hard to envision some conflict among these scales (a city under siege might have high morale, but low satisfaction and adjustment, for instance) or the various dimensions on them, it seems probable that Sun Citians answered the questions generally in a positive manner, as Bultena and Wood said they did.

The question is rather the extent to which the answers represent some degree of denial of their actual self and world perceptions. The community does not force instrumental values upon persons, but it does insist upon a positive outlook. Not to have one is to risk being a social pariah. Hence, there is a rather heavy community investment in happiness, which individuals cannot ignore. If they have feelings that are otherwise they may have difficulty in acknowledging and reporting them.

Denial is a virtually universal human mechanism of psychic defense (protection of the self) which is often useful and even sometimes necessary for survival. We must selectively not attend to some phenomena, and then sometimes deny that they exist, or they will overwhelm us. So the question is not whether Sun Citians are denying certain aspects of their situation, but whether they are paying too high a price in doing so. I think in some instances they are paying such a price. Sadness which cannot be publicly expressed without social discomfort, can easily lead to depression or chemically induced "happiness" at home alone. In a community in which bereavement is common sadness needs to be acceptable at places other than funerals and memorial services.

The cultural climate of the Sun Cities thus has some real assets and some probable liabilities when we consider the need for pastoral counseling and readiness to recognize the need. Need is lessened by the support of friends and some aspects of the community, especially the group life afforded by some of the churches at the time of bereavement, but it is increased by the difficulty the community has in dealing with negative feelings of any kind, especially feelings of sadness. When there is a need for counseling, the community does not easily support a readiness for it, since to acknowledge a need for help represents a kind of failure to live up to the community standards for positive affect. This lack of support of readiness for counseling, when coupled with the reticence of persons reared in the pre-"mental health" era, probably means that many who may need pastoral counseling, or similar services, choose to go without them. Sensitive caregivers and friends can help to develop readiness, when they are alert to these needs.

3. *Stratified Age-Segregated Continuing Care Retirement Communities.* There are many of these communities in existence, and more are coming into being all the time, including many around homeowner communities, such as Sun City, Arizona. Typically, they have three levels of living arrangements, ranging from more or less completely independent in apartments or cottages, through semi-independent, where meal service and other personal services are provided, to nursing home, or "assisted living." Sometimes these three levels are further divided into more fine-grained distinctions, but generally the three are discernable. Although the ethos of these communities is not uniform, the communities have a common feature of being much more heavily influenced by planners and by administrators, and less by the residents, than do homeowner communities. In order to show the influence of the structure of these communities on the lives of the residents, and on their attitude toward pastoral counseling in particular, I shall focus on one life-care community, which has some distinctive, and perhaps even singular, features regarding pastoral care and counseling.

Asbury Methodist Village is a stratified, "life care," retirement community in Gaithersburg, Maryland, which, as its name indicates, is affiliated with the United Methodist Church.

It has about 1000 residents, 500 of whom live independently in apartments, 250 in semi-independent apartments, and 250 in a nursing home arrangement in the Wilson Health Care Center. Asbury has a staff of trained full-time chaplains, one of whom, W. K. "Lucky" Childress, is a supervisor for the Association for Clinical Pastoral Education, which means that there are usually several students, some of whom are advanced, in pastoral care and counseling there as well.

In an interview Childress indicated that about 20 residents, chiefly from the independent apartments, are in pastoral counseling during the course of the year. This counseling tends to be rather long-term as pastoral counseling goes—up to a year or more. This counseling is, of course, in addition to routine pastoral care, and rather short-term counseling which may last two to four sessions. Residents come to the chaplains' offices for counseling, while they generally receive pastoral care in their own residental areas. Residents are made aware that pastoral counseling is available by posted notices in their living areas, by personal contact with the chaplains, and by word of mouth. Childress indicated that perhaps twice as many persons wished to be seen who might be viable candidates, but that staff resources were not available for them. No fee is charged for pastoral counseling.

From our point of view the striking thing is that pastoral counseling is being done rather systematically at Asbury, even though on a relatively small scale—with about 4 percent of the most likely population, those in independent living. The *setting* of the church related facility with a trained chaplain staff whom the residents know personally, generates a set of *expectations* that, through a *shift in relationship,* some alteration in their lives can be effected. *Aims and limitations* are less affected by the context of the retirement center, and are what might be appropriate for a more general population of older persons. In this generation guilt feelings receive considerable attention, as do transitions of aging—losses, despair (death wishes), and body images. I have some question about whether the context perhaps should affect the aims of counseling more, so that it becomes more short-term, allowing for more counselees. Time limited counseling and psychotherapy have sometimes been shown to be as effective as unlimited.

I believe the pastoral counseling being done at Asbury Methodist Village points in the direction of increasing services of this kind to older persons everywhere. Clearly, an encouraging setting with resources brings older persons to take advantage of those resources, overcoming decades of fear and ignorance about personal helping processes.

4. *Summary.* Of the three contexts examined, the age-segregated continuing care retirement community with full chaplaincy services was the most conducive to pastoral counseling, and the homeowner age-segregated community the least conducive, with the age-integrated communities, I believe, falling somewhere in the middle on this continuum. All the factors present in settings like Asbury Methodist Village cannot be replicated in other settings, even if it were desirable to do so, when everthing is taken into account. But more might be done in age-integrated communities to encourage older persons to allow themselves to have some personal problems and to seek appropriate help. More allowance can be made for human frailty by the community, and human possibility by the pastoral workers in the age-segregated Sun Cities without undermining the positive ethos of such places. The ethos, as important as it is in maintaining morale and meaningful activity, can become oppressive for those whose personal world is, at least for the time being, too dark to allow them to participate fully.

Chapter 8

Goals of Pastoral Counseling
with the Elderly

What kinds of outcomes can we really expect from pastoral counseling? Given the general purpose of counseling sketched in chapter 5, the kinds of indications for engaging in counseling presented in chapter 6, and the contexts described in chapter 7, what can be and should be the specific goals which are appropriate in differing instances? Or can goals always be specific? Every experienced counselor knows that often the counseling terminates before formal goals are attained, although in many instances some kind of improvement is noted. It must be acknowledged also, that it is not always appropriate to discuss specific goals of counseling at the outset. Sometimes the person is too distraught to make such discussion meaningful or helpful, although after two or three sessions some discussion of goals is usually appropriate in such cases. In any case, the counselee must finally define the goal in discussion with the counselor, or at least accept the goal proposed. The counselee's explicit or implicit sense of the goal is the closest to the actual goal.

In spite of these apparent limitations I think it is imperative that the counselor have in mind as specific a goal as possible before undertaking formal counseling with the elderly, even though this goal may change. Only by this effort can full responsibility be taken for the counseling, a determination be made about whether counseling should be undertaken at all, and if so what form it should take.

I shall present some goals which I think are appropriate for counseling older persons, and then a model of counseling which I think is the most useful for attaining these.

1. *Principal Goals of Pastoral Counseling with the Elderly.*

These goals are not completely exhaustive, but I think they are appropriate in most instances, and some may be combined, as indeed the first one must be combined with another to be effective.

a. Do no harm. The reader may believe that this point can be assumed, and indeed, pastoral theologians often do so when discussing helping procedures. Since we are discussing a mode of helping about which much doubt and ambivalence exists—the pastoral counseling of the elderly—I am not assuming it, even though most of the doubt is about the matter of wasting time rather than doing harm.

The essential thing is to remember to avoid high risk procedures with the elderly when engaging in pastoral counseling. These are basically of three kinds. The first is that of attempting to get older persons to face personal issues arising from long buried memories which may be so disturbing that they cannot be helpfully dealt with by the counselor in the relatively brief counseling which I think is appropriate in most instances. The second is that of becoming so intensely involved personally with the counselee, and or allowing the counselee to become so involved, that a classical transference/counter-transference develops in which each party, but especially the counselee, may displace intense feelings originating in past relationships, especially with close family members, onto the counselor or counselee. Ordinarily this problem can be avoided by limiting counseling to a few interviews. Arthur H. Becker proposes six interviews, a conservative number in my estimation.[1] I think that ten to twelve interviews for a pastoral counselor with some training, and this includes many parish ministers, is a reasonable limit. This higher limit can provide more time to accomplish appropriate goals, but does entail awareness of transference possibilities on the part of the counselor.

These two possibilities for doing harm are closely related, and frequently occur together. The counselor may uncover intense feelings about a parent, and transference of feelings about that parent develop, even though the counselor may be half the age of the counselee. The result is a situation that the counselor is too deeply involved in to lead the elderly counselee through without serious risk of disintegrative damage to the self.

A third way of doing harm is to engage in pastoral counseling when some other helping mode is actually indicated. These modes might range all the way from surgery to seeing a lawyer, and would-be pastoral counselors need to keep the primary question about whether the person really needs this kind of help in mind. There is a danger that pastoral counseling will be done when not needed, even though the far more prevalent danger is that it will *not* be done when needed.

b. Reduce discomfort/increase comfort. Reducing discomfort may seem to some to be an inadequate goal of pastoral counseling, and perhaps that of increasing comfort (not necessarily quite the same as reducing discomfort) even more inadequate, or actually perverse. To those who have taken to heart the "no pain, no gain" motto of exercise devotees, suggesting that merely reducing discomfort, or pain, or anxiety, or other disagreeable affects, has the ring of giving in to the forces of decadence. To these advocates of effortful striving may be added much of the psychotherapeutic tradition, beginning with Freud himself, who viewed psychoanalysis as a journey to be undertaken in a state of deprivation and psychic stress, before reaching the sought-for plateau of reintegration. To be sure, some tolerance for discomfort may be needed to attain its ultimate reduction, but with older persons this tolerance does not need to be elevated to a positive virtue. Rather, most elderly will have experienced enough suffering in life to persuade them that more is not needed, even if it presumably is necessary for later increase in comfort.

This does not mean that the elderly are incapable of tolerating pain and distress, for most tolerate some of it all the time, and are prepared to continue to do so. But the continuing discomfort of rheumatism and arthritis can be better tolerated if overall comfort is increased by the diminishment of anxiety related to troubles in the family, for instance. In such instances we can see that the increase in comfort in personal life can more than compensate one for lack of reduction in specific, painful, discomfort. Prolonged and intense grief is another great discomfort which can be diminished through counseling, and its reduction alone makes the process worthwhile, even if other distresses remain.

Although we may hope for "growth" in personality through counseling, and I shall be shortly presenting a discussion of such possibilities, I believe that reduction in discomfort and/or increase in comfort is goal enough in many cases. For many spirits over 75 introspection is a wearisome thing, and even for many of "the young old." Often they cannot introspect much. But with some help they can do enough to alleviate some distress, if not enough to prevent its recurrence. A 75-year-old engineer who has focused on the manipulation of the environment all his life can get relief from talking out his tangled relationship with his son, and perhaps alter his behavior a bit. But he cannot completely change his propensities to influence, not very subtly, his son's life.

Another factor which enters into this discussion is the relatively shorter time span which the future represents for the elderly. They may feel that counseling is worthwhile, but only if the gain can be envisioned with some degree of clarity as happening in the near term. Not all do feel this way, but the point is that counseling is often appropriate for those who do— "a cup of cold water" is appropriate ministry for those who thirst, even if our subsequent efforts to guide them in a direction which we prefer are not well received. Just as older persons are sometimes not as much motivated to make the effort to memorize material offered by researchers as are college sophomores, who may believe that their futures depend in some way on their efforts, so the elderly may also find that investment in pastoral counseling may be limited by their sense of encroaching horizons. Nevertheless, I believe that many are willing to make a considerable investment.

c. Enable decision making. Although the phrase "enable decision making" seems rather straightforward, and even conjures visions of calmly deliberating seniors wisely determining their destinies, behind it often lie painful doubt, agonizing obsessing, and grinding anxiety. Often alone, the elderly wonder whether they should move, for instance. If so, should an offer to move in with a daughter's family be taken up? Questions like this and a host of others about crucial life decisions confront many older people every day.

Sometimes these questions involve others, particularly other family members. All too often they are answered without the full participation of the elderly person whose future is being radically affected. Our concern here is to assert the necessity of involving the older person to the fullest extent possible, without denying that whole families may be involved and properly included in the decision-making process. Family counseling may well be helpful in resolving such questions, but if the older person is the one primarily affected, she or he should also be afforded an opportunity for individual pastoral counseling.

In addition to the question of where one should be living, other frequently felt questions which press for resolution in the lives of the elderly are in the areas of finances and health care, and the relationship between the two. Although pastoral counseling cannot alone provide the information needed to make these decisions, counseling can frequently assist in dealing with the anxiety associated with these matters, and so better prepare the elderly to make good use of more expert help to which they may be referred.

Mary, age 83, is a church member who lives alone, with a son living about 35 miles away. Recently, she has experienced some "blackouts" and has been told she needs some expensive diagnostic procedures to discover the cause. Mary carries two Medicare supplement health insurance policies, but upon inquiry, both state they will pay only a small part of the cost beyond Medicare. She does not know what she should do, as she has only meager resources in cash. Should she appeal to her son? She is reluctant to do this because of the tangles in her relationship with him. Should she attempt to borrow money? Should she seek other insurance, and drop what she has? That will not help her with her current medical problem, in any event. A pastoral counselor can help Mary to sift through some of these options while alleviating her anxiety, which is growing and becoming a significant part of the problem. Then a resource person with more expertise in the financial problems of the elderly may be needed to help Mary make final decisions about these matters.

d. Clarification of vocation. Since this topic has been treated rather extensively in chapter 6, I shall not here repeat all that was said there about the need for the vocational counseling of older people. Rather, our focus will be on the question of what, realistically, can we expect to achieve?

I think that one important goal is to help the elderly to think about themselves as being vocationally oriented, so that many issues of self focus (what am I worth, how can I find meaning in life?) can be seen as actually questions about vocation. Thus, what is usually called "insight" or "self-understanding" counseling can be given a new valuation when seen as a vital part, but only a part, of vocational counseling. The vectors of the spirit toward the world of persons and things, and toward the God who calls one to a vocation, must also be duly attended to. When persons troubled about themselves and their relationship to the world about them begin to understand these questions in a vocational framework, meaning is imparted thereby, even if they discover that aspects, or even all, of their vocational aspirations cannot be realized.

Another objective of vocational counseling is to assist persons toward what Sharon Kaufman has called the symbolic continuity of the self in late life with the self one feels oneself to have been.[2] Kaufman has argued convincingly, based on her own research and that of Clark and Anderson, done more than two decades ago, that meaning in late life often depends primarily upon perceived continuity between present and past.[3] Kaufman puts this continuity in terms of self, and that is surely a part of the picture, but it is the self relating to the world vocationally in which the meaning in most of her examples is to be found. Stella, for instance, found meaning in her life through sculpture and painting after her child was killed when she was 40.[4] All of the people in Kaufman's study were middle-class San Franciscans over 70, which may limit the applicability of her findings to similar urban dwellers. Nevertheless, I believe she has furnished us with a central goal to be considered when engaging in vocationally focused counseling.

Assisting older persons to make the adaptive changes often needed to provide them with a sense of vocational continuity becomes an important goal of this kind of counseling in light of the discussion in the foregoing paragraph. Changes come, whether invited or not, and adaptation to change is thus needed, perhaps paradoxically, to provide a sense of continuōus sameness. The Sun City former gift shop operator, Tom, described in chapter 7, translated his sales skills with middle and upper middle-class people into a post-retirement symbolic continuity in selling real estate to the same kind of people. He, along with many others, can furnish clues about how counselors can assist their counselees to make similar symbolic adaptations.

e. Consolidation of self. From the point of view of the formal schema of this chapter, the consolidation of self should be treated as a part of the goal of vocational counseling, since such consolidation always, in principle, has a forward looking valence toward vocation. But the fragmentation and lack of integrity in the sense of regrets, guilt, and shame is often experienced acutely by older persons or emerges as an issue in counseling begun for other reasons. Vocational counseling proper, with its emphasis upon the future, must await some resolution of these issues of lack of cohesion or felt integrity in the self. In such cases reminiscence becomes an important tool, with the limited goal of finding some of the roots of troublesome memories, learning to forgive oneself, and thus, to let those memories go. The forgiveness which is to be found in the Christian gospel is often an explicit catalytic factor in this process. When this is accomplished, vocational counseling can proceed.

Peter G. Coleman, in *Aging and Reminiscence Processes*, has shown both the strengths and limitations of reminiscence, or life review, as a therapeutic tool.[5] Not all persons seem be able to benefit from reminiscence, and some find it repugnant.[6] For those who can reminisce, however, life review can aid self-esteem in the present for those dissatisfied with their pasts.[7] Coleman reminds us that the elderly may still have a dim view of the present, even after counseling, for they have a vested interest in the past, and many feel they are "under moral siege" in the present.[8] Those best adapted are the storytellers who find continuity in their lives.[9] Even when "happiness" seems to elude them in old age, many find life satisfaction in the sense of past achievements. Counseling can help examine the rough places in the past for some, reduce their power, and increase the influence in the present of the positive experiences of the past. From consolidation of the self can come increased life satisfaction, even though vocational and spiritual questions remain. Hence, consolidation of self, spanning past to present, is a quite legitimate goal of pastoral counseling.

f. Reconciliation of family and significant others. Reconciliation is an important goal for pastoral counseling in any age group, but for the elderly it is especially important. Spousal reconciliation is particularly important, as was noted in chapter 6, but also efforts to reconcile elders to their children and sometime friends, when they are estranged, should be made. These points were also discussed as indicators for counseling in chapter 6, so no extended comments will be made here. The procedures to be used in these kinds of reconciliation counseling will often differ markedly, especially when family members are involved and a systems approach is indicated. But we emphasize here that the goal is primarily reconciliation in these differing emphases, although some systems theorists might argue that, even when older members are in the center of conflict, the restoration of the functionality of system is the primary goal. From the point of the view of the elderly, the dominant one in this book, it is reconciliation.

g. Provide a resource for spirit in relation to self. It is difficult to state adequately the goal of pastoral counseling in relationship to spirit, since the spirit's ultimate goal is to return to its creator, after enriching the world and being enriched by it. Pastoral counseling as such cannot necessarily provide all that is needed for the maximum development of the spiritual life. But it is often needed to address the relationship between self and spirit, where the needs of the self can sometimes confound and convolute the vectors of the spirit. Difficulties in the relationship of self and spirit were discussed in chapter 6 under the heading "Self-Identified Focal Spiritual Questions," and not all of it will be repeated.

A minimal goal of pastoral counseling in relation to spirit is that of disentangling the narrow concerns of the self from the spirit. Although spirit and self are always closely connected, the self can, and often does, unduly influence the vectors of the spirit, coloring them with its concerns, which may be grandiose or suffused with unresolved struggles with parental figures, for an instance of a frequent, but not the only, kind of confusion. Yes, even older people do sometimes confuse their own parents with God, and especially their feelings and expectations of their parents may be taken for attitudes toward God. Larger goals for the spiritual life may be explored through pastoral counseling. What forms of prayer may be best suited to a given personality is a proper question for pastoral counseling, for instance. But the pursuit of spiritual growth itself, if the matter of the entanglements of the self have been taken care of, is best left for guidance by a spiritual director, or friend of the spirit, which may continue for a much longer period of time, if less intensively, than is appropriate for pastoral counseling. This might or might not be the same person as the pastoral counselor. *The Practice of Spiritual Direction*, by William A. Barry and William J. Connolly, is a helpful discussion of that topic.[10] Much help can also be gained from well written self-help books on the spiritual life, such as *Living Simply in an Anxious World*, by Robert J. Wicks, or David J. Maitland's *Aging as Counterculture: A Vocation for the Later Years*, a challenge to the elderly to buck cultural trends.[11]

2. *A Cognitive Model for Pastoral Counseling.* At first glance the phrase, "cognitive model" for counseling may seem, as I confess it did to me several years ago when I first encountered it, hopelessly intellectualized to be of any use in pastoral counseling, trained as I was in Rogerian and Freudian approaches. However, I have come to appreciate possibilities of getting to the emotional life through thought processes, which is what the cognitive model is basically all about. Thinking does not in this context mean abstract thought, but very concrete expression for the most part, and includes what Freud called "primary process thinking," or very primitive, for the most part unconscious, wish oriented thinking, or what Richard S. Lazarus has called "unconscious appraisal."[12]

In taking this position I am not trying to provide some kind of answer to the chicken/egg question of whether thinking precedes emotion developmentally, or whether it requires language for expression, as this question does not have to be addressed in order for cognitively oriented clinical intervention to be effective. The issue that concerns us is, rather, whether the "appraisal" that is made of the situation is in some sense a cognitive appraisal and thus accessible to verbal intervention. I am affirming that we do make such cognitive appraisals and that they are accessible for constructive change. Aaron T. Beck was the pioneer and still is the leader in the cognitive therapy movement, especially as it was developed as a treatment for depression, although Albert Ellis was moving along a similar track about the same time.[13]

Before providing some description of the cognitive model (and a modification of it called cognitive-behavioral, which incorporates some behavioral emphases.[14]), I need to say that I do not regard it as the only model for doing pastoral counseling with the elderly. In one of the few studies of outcome of psychotherapy done with older people, L. W. Thompson and colleagues found in 1987 that cognitive, brief psychodynamic and behavioral approaches resulted in some improvement in depression, while a waitlisted group showed none.[15] Thus, no claim can be made that the cognitive model is the best. Rather, I claim that it is more understandable and plausible than the others, and can be taught and learned readily enough within a relatively brief span of time to be used responsibly, albeit in a limited fashion. I present this model with a "flavor" of psychodynamics, which I think enriches it.

Arthur Freeman and Vincent Greenwood have characterized cognitive therapy as "a relatively short term form of psychotherapy that is active, directive, and collaborative between patient and therapist."[16] Beck himself, in a recent retrospective article, has asserted the effectiveness of cognitive therapy in unipolar depression, anxiety disorders, and panic disorder, basing his assertion on numerous studies.[17] As indicated above, the goal of cognitive therapy or counseling is to deal with affective disorders through cognitive strategies. It is often combined with behavior techniques, such as giving "homework" to alter one's relational patterns, a move which I think is often a good one.

According to Freeman and Greenwood, Beck posited three factors in emotion: the cognitive triad (idiosyncratic negative view of self, world and future), cognitive distortions (such as all or nothing thinking, catastrophizing, and overgeneralization), and schema (the underlying assumptions about the self and the world).[18] Most counseling deals with the distortions only, even though, theoretically, the schema needs to be changed for more lasting help.

Some discussion of some frequently occurring distortions will, I think, help us to see that these are problems frequently besetting older people, and that the cognitive model may be an appropriate one. In addition to those mentioned above, others are selective abstraction, disqualifying the positive, arbitrary inference, magnification or minimization, should/must/ought statements, labeling and mislabeling, and personalization (paranoid thinking). It may appear that persons suffering from these problems in thinking need a course in logic! Indeed, although such a course might help, the distortions are believed to be due to the irrational belief system embodied in the schema beneath the surface.[19] Much of the distortions are differing ways of perceiving the environment in keeping with the distortions in the schema. Thus, selective abstraction means choosing only those pieces of evidence that support one's distortions. Disqualifying the positive means disregarding evidence that doesn't fit one's negative presuppositions. Arbitrary inference concerns interpreting human behavior in a uniformly rejecting way. Magnification or minimization means misjudging the personal significance of what one is experiencing. Should/must/ought statements result from internalization of expectations of rejection, similar to the way in which we think of the Freudian superego. Labeling and mislabeling both are efforts to control the environment. Personalization attributes negative intentions to the impersonal environment in accordance with the underlying worldview.

No one has all these attributes, happily. But many of the elderly have some of them. It can be seen, I think, that if we could radically alter, or even modify, these kinds of distortions in the thinking of the elderly, much will be achieved. Efforts to change the thinking distortions posited by the cognitive model and the goals of pastoral counseling of the elderly are quite congruent. Meyer D. Glanz has provided evidence of the effectiveness of the cognitive model with the elderly in his "Cognitive Therapy with the Elderly."[20] The model provides a solid base for counseling, even if the procedures associated with it may need supplementing, as I think they do in some instances. These and other matters pertaining to procedures will be discussed in the chapter which follows.

3. *Summary.* The goals of pastoral counseling with the elderly have been presented as doing no harm, reducing discomfort, enabling decision making, clarifying vocation, consolidating the self, reconciling with family and friends, and providing a resource for the spirit in relation to the self. A model of cognition as providing access to the emotional life, as developed by Aaron T. Beck and his associates, was presented and discussed. Initially developed to facilitate the treatment of depression, this model has since been found to be applicable to broad areas of emotional distress. The cognitive model will be the principal model proposed to serve as a base for achieving the goals of pastoral counseling.

Chapter 9

Procedures for Pastoral Counseling with the Elderly

In this final chapter some procedural strategies will be presented and discussed. Several of these are derived from cognitive models of counseling and therapy either directly or indirectly, while others, though in my estimation compatible with the cognitive model, are developed from other sources. This last point is especially true of the procedures presented under the seventh and final section, "Some Particular Situations and Problems."

The first six procedures presented are intended for use with individuals who are able to engage in some effortful self-inspection. Before beginning to use them, the pastoral counselor needs to acquaint the counselee with the main features of cognitive counseling—in particular the approach to the emotions through thinking. The counselee's full collaboration in the counseling is solicited, and as complete an understanding of the processes as may be possible at the outset is provided. As indicated in chapter 2, some older people, especially many of those born around 1920 or before, have trouble engaging in counseling because of its connotations of strangeness or craziness. But many of these are able to engage in fruitful counseling, given the right setting and counselor. They have become ready through education and experience. These procedures are intended to be used to try to help such individuals in this cohort, as well as those who may be younger.

The procedures sketched in the last section are intended for various groupings of persons as couples, families, and peer groups, and for those, especially some older couples in marital distress, who have difficulty with introspective approaches to counseling.

88

The first six procedures are best utilized by parish ministers with training in pastoral care and counseling at least a significant step beyond a seminary introductory course, or first unit of clinical pastoral education, or by lay persons with comparable training. Experience, of course, is also useful, if it is duly reflected upon and assimilated. The procedures are not absolutely discrete, and although the sequencing of the presentation provides some guidance about sequence, often they will need to be intermixed. The counselor always needs to be caring and interested, and to communicate these characteristics.

1. *Conveying Empathic Understanding.* This is actually the first principle of all pastoral care and counseling. But because this is so does not reduce the need for restating it here. Conveying that the counselor has some sense of how the older person is experiencing self and world, and that she or he can accept that experience, is just as vital as with any other age group. Empathy, a "feeling into" the thoughts, feelings, and experiences of another, without directly experiencing them as one's own (as contrasted with sympathy, the "feeling with" another on the basis of one's own similar experience), provides the basis of several important features of counseling.

First, it builds trust which, to be sure, must already be present in a significant degree for pastoral counseling to begin. But trust must be maintained and enhanced by empathy in counseling as well as before it starts. When we perceive that someone is really making the effort to attend to us and can communicate to us an accepting understanding of our own experience, even if this communication is only an approximation conveyed through body language and metaphor, our trust level increases. As it increases the relationship can then more readily tolerate other kinds of responses and initiatives by the counselor which will be necessary for effective counseling. Questions sometimes probe like a needle, and even gentle interpretations often produce some shame and anger. Only a high trust level provided by empathy conveyed frequently can sustain counseling through these prickles to a fruitful end.

Empathy and acceptance enable the counselee to proceed to deeper levels of consciousness as one experiences greater apprehension of oneself. This is especially true if the counselor can use metaphors which touch the unspoken thoughts and feelings as well as the spoken communication of the counselee. Being understood seems to help the counselee to get in touch with more and more aspects of self which may have been beneath consciousness. Meyer D. Glantz, in his essay, "Cognitive Therapy with the Elderly," stresses the point that the elderly need to be especially encouraged to express deeper feelings, pointing out that many consciously constrict their range of emotions, mislabel them, or feel that they have no right to express them. "Encouraging and giving 'permission' for patients to feel and express the full range of emotions is very beneficial."[1]

In a seeming paradox empathy also enables one to become a more discerning judge of oneself. As the counselee hears what he or she is communicating conveyed back in an accepting manner, frequently that person will experience a mildly negative reaction: "This is not what I want to be, even if it is what I am." In this way, empathy is a facilitator of change in personal response patterns.

It ought to be noted here that attempts to convey empathy, unless sensitively done, can sometimes seem patronizing, especially to older men who are not accustomed to having their feelings discussed, and who may have intellectual defenses against the awareness of emotions. Nevertheless, empathy with a light metaphorical touch can loosen constricted self-systems, as in the following exchange:

> Sam: I don't know what to do with myself with Bess gone, I just sit and stare at the TV a lot.
> Counselor: There's a big vacancy in your life, inside as well as outside.
> Sam: Yeah, it like there's a hole in me.

Other points about empathy could be made, but perhaps these will suffice to show its importance. It is not derived from cognitive models of helping, but from the older client, or person-centered, model developed by Carl R. Rogers and brought into pastoral counseling by Carroll Wise and Seward Hiltner.[2] More recently the work of psychoanalytic self theorist Heinz

Kohut has served to reinforce the importance of empathy within the pastoral care movement.

Nevertheless, empathy is quite compatible with cognitive approaches if we realize that, in order to focus more clearly on thoughts, troublesome negative feelings, especially anxiety, anger and fear, will often have to be addressed directly with empathy. This is especially true at the outset of counseling, but also intermittently throughout its course. The general principle of pastoral (and other kinds of) counseling that feelings must first be attended to before thoughts can be clarified still holds, especially with older people, whose emotions sometimes have become hard to express and need particular encouragement.

I shall not dwell further on the need for empathy, but its importance cannot be overestimated. It is a kind of repeated bass line above which the melodies of counseling are played.

2. *Questioning the Evidence.* If empathy is arcane and ripe for caricature, questioning seems by contrast the epitome of common sense. Questioning is what about four-fifths of seminarians do when encountering their first opportunity for pastoral care. "How long have you felt this way?" "Does your brother feel the same way about you?" "Have you tried telling her how you feel?" These are examples of the kinds of fact-oriented questions that beginners, relying on common sense, may ask. They are not necessarily inappropriate, if they do not become a monotonous pattern, but they are not the kinds of questions indicated by "questioning the evidence." The evidence refers to the grounds that the counselee has for the negative construal of her or his life situation. Do the facts actually warrant the often very deeply painful feelings associated with the way the situation is perceived? Often, we find that they do not, and by showing this lack of foundation we may begin to help the sufferer to see that the disastrous cues she or he has been taking from the presumably catastrophic situation are not warranted by the facts.

The reader may be thinking, though, that often in the lives of the elderly the facts do warrant a decidedly negative construal. The health-care system really is a mess and the elderly are caught in it; they have suffered many losses including often that of their spouse; they are regarded as superfluous misfits by many in society. While this is true in many instances, still there are usually elements of idiosyncratic exaggeration even in the worst of scenarios. These can be gently pointed out. Especially important is it to point out and question elements of self-blame which occur repeatedly and irrationally in the "stories" of older people. It is not that all self-blame is inappropriate. As Howard W. Stone has pointed out, if irrational self-blame is reduced, appropriate self-blame, or actual sin, may be confronted.[3]

The key issue is to help the individual to begin to identify the *cognitive appraisal* which she or he has been making by which the situation has been construed as overwhelming, hopeless, or otherwise threatening the coherence of self and spirit. Questioning the evidence alone will not produce a lot of positive change, but it begins to loosen up impacted patterns of thought stemming from the negative cognitive schema underneath. As a part of identifying cognitive appraisal, a *life review* may be indicated through encouraging reminiscence, but we need to recall that not all older persons seem to profit from it, especially those with very troubled pasts.

There are, of course, cases in which the bleakness of attitude and outlook seem to correspond to the actualities, when to have integrity does mean, if not to despair, at least to find no comfort in the prospects of this world. In these cases, not further counseling, but ongoing sustaining pastoral care, is appropriate.

3. *Reinterpretation.* As this term clearly implies, there is no uninterpreted experience, and a part of the task of counseling is to reinterpret some key elements in it. This is the next step beyond questioning the evidence—that of suggesting alternative construals and understandings. Many of the techniques and strategies proposed by cognitive therapists are of this kind, which they generally refer to as restructuring cognition. The following reinterpretative strategies are examples of those employed in cognitive therapy and counseling, but they are not exhaustive, either of those employed, or of those that might be constructed for particular problems and issues.

a. Reattribution.[4] This is the replacing of inappropriate

self-blame statements ("It's all my fault") with a more accurate distribution of responsibility among all relevant parties and non-human factors. While it is important for persons to accept realistic responsibility, the attribution of unrealistic responsibility to oneself is much more common among older people than the reverse of too little responsibility, especially among those prone to depression. In addition to reviewing the facts, the counselor may be able to show that the person has different criteria for assigning responsibility to him or her self as compared with the criteria used in assigning responsibility to others, resulting in a double standard, and challenging the belief that the person is 100 percent to blame for any negative consequences.[5] Reattribution has a parallel in more traditional dynamic psychotherapies in the effort to replace superego dominance with ego dominance, via a more circuitous approach through childhood experience.

b. De-Catastrophizing. This technique focuses upon raising the "what if" questions about what will happen if the worst-case possibility comes true. Again, with older people catastrophe in the forms of incapacitation, suffering, and death may be possible outcomes of the flow of current events. Even then, these are not certain in the near term in most cases. So often a catastrophic schema that tells the person that the worst is always about to occur is underlying this kind of thinking and needs challenging. What, indeed, if Parkinsonism is progressive, and life always fatal? Although this kind of intervention can be abused as "bright-siding," or looking for the silver lining with people for whom such messages only increase despair, still it is often a necessary corrective to thinking already tinted with darkness. The temptation to bring in the love of God at points like this before the counselee can really attend to that message must be resisted, however.

c. Fantasized consequences. Sometimes the counselee cannot easily verbalize what is troubling him or her. In such instances it may be helpful to try to get the person to imagine what is going to happen. In many instances a worst case scenario emerges, of the sort discussed above in "De-Catastrophizing." Then the fantasy can be accordingly challenged, when appropriate.

d. Advantages and disadvantages. The counselee lists the advantages and disadvantages of a belief or behavior they have. In this way counselees can gain some perspective on crucial aspects of themselves. This technique is an example of "scaling," a larger term for any approach to viewing life on a continuum rather than "all or nothing," as is the inclination of many. Making lists is not for everyone, but for many who have used approaches like this in the past to solving problems, it can be helpful.

e. Turning adversity to advantage. This kind of approach can only be taken when there is an actual advantage potentially hidden in adversity. Care should be taken not to try to manufacture these where none exists. Nevertheless, counselors need to be alert for opportunities to suggest instances where this approach can work, even though they do not go as far as one of the prime exemplars, Milton's Satan, who, finding himself in hell, comforted himself thus, "The mind is its own place, and in itself can make a heaven of hell, a hell of heaven." (*Paradise Lost*, Book I) For those who believe that only darkness and pain lie ahead, the possibility of less dismal prospects and opportunity can be a positive revelation.

f. Labeling of distortions. If labeling and mislabeling are often a part of the problem, so the labeling of distortions for what they are can become a part of the solution. Such labeling gives the counselee a needed sense of power over the distortions that have caused her or him difficulty. Being able to say, "I was making mountains out of molehills when I reacted with panic every time I got a letter from the government," can provide a part of a more solid platform for dealing not only with the mail, but many other anxiety provoking situations, as well.

g. Paradox or exaggeration—humor. The use of exaggeration or paradox to suggest the incongruence or lack of cogency of the counselee's thinking may be effective in some instances. Aaron Beck rightly cautions that, ". . . even if the patient apparently laughs or smiles, it is important to determine whether the patient construed the humor in a negative way."[6] He also says that some helpers are not prepared to use humor, and that the helper must be clear that the target of the humor is the counselee's ideas, not the person.[7] In light of these cautions I can only recommend the use of this technique for well-established relationships which enjoy a high level of trust.

h. Scaling. For the counselee who sees most things as all or nothing, scaling is a name for the general approach of attempting to help the counselee to think of them, and thus to see them, on a continuum. Procedure "d," dealing with making lists of advantages and disadvantages of a particular belief or behavior, is an example of scaling. Admittedly, some things in life are not on a continuum. You are either safe or out in baseball; you are either pregnant or you are not. Yet much of the stimuli which cause difficulty to older persons are on continuums. Losses are temporarily overwhelming, but even with them, much abides. The glass may actually be half full, or nearly so, even though it appears empty.

This procedure and some others may sometimes appear as "positive thinking," in the sense that the reality of the situation will not really be adequately reflected. Beck and his colleagues are aware of this potential abuse and caution against making more of the positive than the situation will actually sustain, a position I strongly endorse.

A procedure used in cognitive therapy, called by Freeman "downward arrow," is designed to lead to progressively deeper levels of consciousness through guided association by means of leading questions to the schema.[8] I do not advocate the use of this procedure, except by those with considerable experience and a time frame long enough to follow it up, should the schema level turn out to involve troubling materials, which in a psychodynamic frame of reference might well be called unconscious.

4. *Constructing a Life Strategy: New Directions for Self/ Spirit.* Reinterpretation focuses on the past, mostly the recent past, but nevertheless the past. Now the counseling process turns toward the future and begins to try to construct some new strategies and cognitive approaches to revitalizing the self-spirit relationship.

a. Examining options and alternatives. Although this procedure begins as a part of reinterpretation, since many persons view their options in an unrealistically constricted fashion, it is best viewed as part of new directions. As some of the debris is

being cleared away from the thinking patterns of the counselee, what new options are now emerging? These need to be
explored with care and in some detail.

b. Cognitive rehearsal. In this procedure the counselee is
asked to envisage her or himself engaging in a new behavior at
the fully conscious reality oriented level of functioning. Ath-
letes often use this technique to enhance performance—lifting
more weights, jumping higher, catching a longer pass. For
older people this kind of rehearsal is often focused on a new
kind of volunteer activity or interpersonal setting. Attention
needs to be paid to details in this kind of procedure, and patience on the part of the counselor is essential, as it may be
difficult for some older counselees to engage fully in this kind
of exercise.

Anne Jones, age 77, after a life as a small-business woman,
wife and mother, had found herself widowed, alone, and having
suffered a mild stroke, somewhat at risk for cardiovascular accidents. She considered moving into a continuing care community, but hesitated, with anxiety mounting. Her discomfort and
agitation came to the attention of her pastor, who initiated contact that led to counseling. After three interviews and some life
review it became evident that Anne feared the loss of her selfhood in the continuing care community, which she perceived
as making her dependent and blunting her keen mind. The
pastor led her through some very detailed cognitive rehearsals
of what life in the new community would be like, which helped
her to make the decision to move in.

c. Replacement imagery. In contrast to the reality oriented cognitive rehearsals advocated above, replacing imagery
touches the world of dreams, the semiconscious, and the unconscious. This means that imagery plays a powerful role in the life
of the self, and that involving it in counseling must be done with
considerable caution. I agree with the following strong statement by Christie Cozad Neuger, whose Ph.D. dissertation
dealt with imagery in pastoral counseling:

> Imagination work in which the power of image is not
> taken seriously can cause considerable damage. Be-
> cause of its ability to both reintegrate and disrupt,

there are times when it should not be used at all (for example, with people who are psychotic or with people who have difficulty differentiating reality from imagination). Imagery techniques, particularly extended fantasy techniques, *should not be used.*[9]

Nevertheless, there is a place for the use of replacement imagery in pastoral counseling, as Neuger also strongly avers. This is so even with the elderly, who may be in even more jeopardy of having images manipulated than other age groups. One general criterion is whether the counselee presents the imagery as a problem on her or his own initiative (given also a lack of psychosis or known organic impairment). Troublesome anxiety-laden dreams are often the form in which these are brought, although others are possible, such as the waking image of a deceased spouse who, dead for some time, appears in surroundings identified with the spouse. In cases of these kinds of images discussion of the meaning in the context of a warm yet rationally focused relationship with a counselor can sometimes alter the image in the dream from one of threat to one of comfort, or at least neutrality. In other instances, where the image of the deceased is a part of grief that is stuck or "frozen," the image ceases to present itself as such, even though the memory of the spouse continues to be cherished in other ways.

It should be noted here that images of the deceased are often a part of recent bereavement, and will usually disappear as time passes and grief progresses. As Neuger has observed, it may be confusing to the recently bereaved to focus on images in pastoral counseling, since images of the deceased may be a part of a psyche destabilized by loss.[10]

From the point of view of cognitive theory, fantasy provides some freedom from a reality orientation to which a counselee may be too closely bound. By guiding positive changes in imagery, which are nevertheless linked to images already present, the counselor may aid in reducing or eliminating the anxiety entangled in the image. Harsh and demanding parental and/or divine figures can become more benign, supportive and loving. Experiences hard to find names for can be touched and sometimes transformed through imagery. Depressed persons have been found to benefit from guided imagery, as have those in pain, those with cancer, and those with phobias.[11]

Admittedly, the points suggested in the foregoing paragraph seem to come close to contradicting the cautions voiced earlier about using imagery techniques. Indeed, I think they do come close. It is clear that highly structured imagery techniques, such as Guided Affective Imagery, advocated by Hanscarl Leuner, should be avoided in short-term pastoral counseling (even though they may be helpful in other contexts). Approaches which attempt to build upon images already present, and carefully selected alternative images may be used, even though with older people the risk may be somewhat higher, if the self structure has become fragile.

Robert Wilson, age 75, began to drink too much after his wife died, caught himself, went through alcohol rehabilitation and came out dry, but mildly depressed and somewhat anxious. He was referred by his rehabilitation counselor, who thought there was a problem of meaning in his life, to a local counseling center for pastoral counseling. After beginning counseling, Robert began to have dreams in which a woman, or women, seemed to menace him much like a witch in a fairy tale. Only a little probing was needed for him to discern that the "witch" was his perception of both his mother and his wife, whom he had split into a composite good woman and bad woman, who was now haunting his dreams and making him anxious during waking hours. When these women were alive he had managed to control his underlying fear that they might rob him of his masculine identity, but now that they were gone, they were "succeeding."

The counselor discovered that he also had some genuine positive feelings about both women which were being for the moment submerged. Some cognitive restructuring helped to show him that his life need not be dominated by fear of apparitions, and positive memories of his wife, encouraged by the counselor, began to surface. The "witch" disappeared. Occasionally, a woman appeared in his dreams to whom he was drawn and who seemed to point the way ahead for him. In this case the counselor stopped short of "guiding" the image, but did influence the course of counseling by relating to dream imagery.

5. *Behavioral Strategies and "Homework."* These strategies are an integral part of the counseling. They serve both the purpose of providing grist for the counseling mill and that of providing possible longer-term beneficial activities. While not all those suggested should be tried with any one counselee, usually one or more will be appropriate.

a. Active scheduling. This strategy can be especially beneficial to many older persons who may have fallen into a pattern of allowing the hours and minutes to merge without much thought. Active scheduling may be applied to counseling appointments for a starter, but can be expanded to include many other activities. Planning the counselee's daily schedule is a worthwhile component of counseling, especially if the person has allowed her or his life to become too disorganized and unstructured. If possible, activities which are interpersonal in character in which self-esteem is likely to be enhanced, activities in which the competence and relative independence can be demonstrated, and some leisure time activities should be scheduled. For those for whom worry and anxiety are special problems, time can be set aside for worry during the day, and the admonition given only to worry during these times and no others.[12]

Care should be taken not to press mildly depressed persons too soon in counseling to actively schedule worry time (and other activities). They may be too depressed to carry these out, and hence, scheduling activities becomes another occasion of failure. Nevertheless, when sensitively negotiated with the counselee, active scheduling can be a very effective means of helping, especially for those prone to depression.

b. Mastery and pleasure ratings. For some older counselees, I think probably a minority, but a significant minority, active scheduling can be used not only to identify helpful activities but to grade them according to the degree of mastery and gratification they afford. Grading will then make it possible to measure increases in competence and pleasure. This procedure would seem to be especially effective with persons who still find that their symbolic self-continuity requires current evidence of achievement.

There is, of course, the risk that decreases, rather than increases, in mastery and pleasure ratings may be found, and may then result in increasing depression or anxiety, although in some cases these apparently dismal results may prod both counselor and counselee to search for new pathways toward meaning which are more appropriate. The golf score may go up, so to speak, resulting in a partial shift to more rewarding volunteer activities which enhance the welfare of others.

c. Behavioral rehearsal, or role playing. In this procedure cognitive rehearsal is carried the further step to actually acting out the envisaged activity which represents a constructive change. This kind of rehearsal may be carried out in the counseling hour itself, or it may be rehearsed as homework (I note here that cognitive rehearsal can also be utilized as homework). If used as homework, the counselee will need to imagine the other person or persons responding to them in the role play. In some instances it may be possible to enlist the services of a close family member or friend who is not directly involved in the conflict situation to assist in the role play. After rehearsal, the behavior can be tried out in the actual situation, and then discussed in counseling.

The kinds of situations for which behavioral rehearsal may be indicated are especially those involving seemingly awkward or emotionally painful interpersonal relations. In earlier life these frequently revolve around scenes in an office with the "boss," or fellow workers. With older persons they may involve other persons in volunteer agencies or church committees, and with government bureaucrats whose cooperation is needed.

For more detail about behavioral rehearsal procedures, consult Howard W. Stone's *Using Behavioral Methods in Pastoral Counseling.*[13] Some of Stone's suggestions, such as staged desensitization procedures, may be too complex for short-term counseling with the elderly, but others, even "thought stopping" to cope with obsessional thoughts, through learning to say "Stop!" when such thoughts occur, may be applicable.

Very careful selection of these techniques is advised, should they be thought to be needed.

  d. Bibliotherapy. Supplementary reading has often accompanied pastoral care and counseling in many forms. It seems especially appropriate when a cognitive model is being utilized in which new information is regarded as being capable of helping to modify attitudes and emotionally loaded thinking. Rather than suggesting specific titles here, I wish to stress the importance of the counselor's sensitivity to the needs and capabilities of the particular counselee in recommending books. Arthur Freeman has recommended texts ranging from Beck's scientific *Cognitive Therapy and the Emotional Disorders* (1976) to self-help books like D. D. Burns' *Feeling Good* (1980). Indeed, Beck is a good writer and many counselees with some background could profit from reading him, while others may find lighter works like Burns more appealing.

  e. Relaxation, breathing, and meditation. Some persons are quite anxious at the outset of counseling and can benefit from relaxation, and especially breathing exercises. These can be done at first in counseling sessions, but then as homework. Meditation as a long-term practice is properly a part of the devotional life and spiritual direction, but as a short-term measure it may be helpfully used as an adjunct to counseling. Texts for meditation should be carefully chosen, again, in the light of the counselor's knowledge of the counselee.

  f. *In vivo* work. Direct modeling of behavior on the part of the counselor in the setting or settings that cause trouble may be very effective in cases of anxiety. Developed as a part of treatment for phobias, especially agoraphobia, in behavior therapy, the accompanying of the counselee to the context of place and person which triggers anxiety can be both reassuring and demonstrative of approaches to coping with the frightening stimuli. Pastoral counselors have an even better entrée into the lives of their counselees than do other counselors, so it is appropriate for them to take advantage of their ability to accompany their older counselees into difficult venues.

  In concluding this section on behavioral rehearsal and homework I should like to stress the point that each homework assignment needs to be tailored to the needs of the individual.

Also, the reason for assigning homework needs to be carefully explained. Beck has underscored both points, urging the therapist to clarify the reasons for the homework assignment. "The therapist and the patient formulate the homework assignments together. This strategy allows the therapist to shape the homework to the individual's situation."[14] Only if the counselee is fully committed to the effectiveness of the homework, will it be likely in fact to prove effective.

6. *Consolidation.* By consolidation is meant that some effort needs to be made to pull together the gains, and to identify areas where goals were not achieved. The reader may think that such a move on the part of the counselor and the counselee can be taken for granted. But much counseling is unfortunately terminated without much or any attention to the question of whether the goal or goals were achieved, what might be done at another time, and what probably will just have to be put up with. Sometimes the goal will have been only minimally achieved, if for instance, the goal was to attain more vocational clarity, where new directional signs may be quite tentative. But even in such instances other vectors of the spirit may have been affected positively or negatively. So these relational vectors, touching, when pertinent, spouses, parents, children, friends, the community, need to be at least briefly reviewed. Sometimes, it will be rather clear that the principal goal has been achieved—if that was to make a certain kind of decision or to reduce discomfort. In other instances it may not be so immediately clear. Has there been enough attention to the cognitive distortions underlying a depressive tendency to prevent the recurrence of mild depression that might be worse next time? Has the anxiety that had substantially immobilized a 75-year-old been not only reduced but sufficiently addressed so that it is less likely to recur? These and other such questions need attention by both counselor and counselee.

Terminating the relationship and its effects on the counselee need also to be addressed at least briefly as a part of the consolidation procedure. Although termination should not be as big an issue in the relatively short-term counseling proposed in this volume, since transference is not developed, it needs to be explicitly addressed at the end of the counseling series, so that the elderly counselee has an opportunity to express thoughts and feelings about it, and the counselor as well.

7. *Some Particular Situations and Problems.* All the foregoing procedures assume that the pastoral counselor is counseling an individual older person who is able and willing to enter into a dialogue about her or himself. Yet several other kinds of situations and possibilities for counseling often present themselves to the caregiver of the elderly. Counseling couples, families, and groups are the most frequently encountered. Of these I shall discuss only the counseling of couples in some detail, while sketching approaches to family and groups, as these require, in my opinion, additional training in order to be effective.

a. Counseling couples. In recent years many pastoral caregivers have come to think of using family systems models when counseling couples. Indeed, this is a possibility, even though other family members are not present in the counseling. However, it is quite legitimate to use other models, including the cognitive model, in counseling couples. Epstein and Baucom have shown how the cognitive model may be effectively employed in marital counseling. I shall present some of the main elements in their approach.

"A cognitive-behavioral approach to marital problems focuses on how spouses often process information about their relationships inappropriately, either deriving invalid conclusions about events, or evaluating those events according to unreasonable standards."[15] Some of these difficulties may be related to the way the two sexes have been socialized in our culture (or perhaps in most cultures), but many are due to idiosyncratic distortions in thinking.

Epstein and Baucom believe that five types of cognitions play a role in marital problems: assumptions, standards, perceptions, attributions, and expectancies.[16] *Assumptions* that affect marriages the most are *personae* typical for someone who is a "husband" or a "wife." These assumptions include both a set of characteristics and a set of assumed correlations among them. Those that cannot be observed among the presumed correlates are inferred to be present nonetheless. For instance, a man who works long hours may be inferred to care for his family, although this inference may be false.[17] *Scripts* about how husband and wife interact include assumptions about sequences of events that occur between partners. Invalid assumptions and flawed scripts produce dysfunctional relationships in marriage.[18]

Standards refer to the characteristics marital partners think their partners should have. Standards are not necessarily dysfunctional, but become so when they become extreme, even if failures to live up to them are evaluated with highly charged reactions. Day-to-day chipping away at unmet standards as well as assumptions closely related to intimate, day-to-day relationships, have been found to be highly correlated to marital distress.[19]

Perceptions are an active, rather than a passive, aspect of receiving information. Attention is selective, and depends in some measure on cognitive structures, emotional states, level of fatigue, and prior experiences in similar situations. Inferences made from thusly colored perceptions play a significant role in marital discord. Further, communications between spouses are subject to "sentiment override," based on one's overall feeling about the spouse, rather than the content of the communication. When things are going sour, spouses tend to track one another's communications negatively, selectively attending to the expected negative aspects of interactions.[20]

Attributions refer to our efforts to make sense of our lives by attributing to human agents events which often baffle and trouble us, and in this context especially to spouses. Distressed spouses tend to see the causes of their partners negative behaviors as due to enduring global character traits, such as selfishness, rather than specific mistakes or limited defects. If the negative attributions are accurate, some other form of helping than cognitive restructuring is probably in order.

Both *outcome expectancies* (the results of given actions) and *efficacy expectancies* (the prediction of one's ability to carry out actions) affect marriages. Expectancies may be accurate or inaccurate, and degree of accuracy is a factor in marital dissatisfaction. Even more involved is a low level of efficacy expectancy, which means that spouses do not have much confidence in their ability to work out their problems, and that counselors will have to change that expectancy if counseling is to succeed.[21]

The long marriages which some older people have are particularly liable to be troubled by these possibilities for cognitive distortion, since they tend to be cumulative. Low and false expectations follow from questionable assumptions about spouses and spouse roles, unrealistic standards, emotion and thought-laden perceptions, and negative attributions. These processes, when they have the momentum of years, can be difficult indeed to turn around, but often can be. On the other hand, new marriages between older persons can also present difficulties in all five of the cognitive areas, since these have been developed separately earlier in life. In both kinds of situations a chronic illness affecting one spouse and placing the other in the role of caregiver can exacerbate existing tensions, as both partners experience resentments and often compensations for resentments.

Counseling procedures based on this model must start with an effort to assess the current functioning of the cognitive areas. Both individual and conjoint interviews can help in this process. Conjoint interviews particularly give the counselor an opportunity to test some ideas by intervening at appropriate times.

The general goal of marriage counseling relying on this model is to increase the number and quality of positive exchanges and decrease the negative ones. Thus, once some sense of the pattern of exchange has been obtained and discussed, some behavioral efforts to change it can be made. Sometimes these can begin with even small changes in the direction of doing something intended to enhance the well-being of the other spouse, perhaps on an alternating daily basis. Other techniques include such devices as checklists of positive and negative behaviors, and the effort to alter these gradually over time. Although these may sound mechanical, they have the advantage of being perceived by many older persons as belonging in the real world in which they live. They require neither deep introspection or arcane imagining. Many of the same procedures suggested in counseling individuals also apply with couples, with necessary changes being made. Various kinds of cognitive and behavioral rehearsal, as well as "homework" will be particularly useful.

Elizabeth, 80, and Robert, 81, married 51 years, have just moved into a new apartment at Green Hills, a multilevel continuing care retirement community. Robert's Parkinsonism has been an increasingly troublesome matter for both of them, in spite of improving medications. He has become increasingly dependent on Elizabeth, and now their new apartment, though pleasant enough, has much less space than their free-standing home that they have just sold, placing them much of the time in close proximity. Both lack of space and dependency violate deep assumptions about husband and wife roles, coloring perceptions of one another negatively and sometimes leading to false attributions and blame. Neither feels they are meeting standards and experience some shame. Robert can no longer fulfill all the aspects of his "husband" role, and Elizabeth's irritation with Robert's failings and self-pity violate her self-image as a nurturer. These factors are precipitators of depression and strife.

The chaplain at Green Hills noticed that Elizabeth and Robert seemed rather sullen and mildly depressed when she encountered them on the grounds, in contrast to their seeming good spirits when she had first met them. She made a call on them in their apartment and discovered, after some initial cover-up, that they were indeed hurting. Counseling was initiated, and cooperative efforts soon identified some of the cognitive factors mentioned above. The couple agreed to make lists of things each were doing that irritated the other, and also of things about themselves that they would like to change, and felt could be changed. These lists were discussed and some changes to adapt to the smaller quarters were initiated, and some others designed to help Robert accept some dependency, while maintaining his functioning independence in other ways. These changes helped enough to reduce significantly the discomfort level of both, even though some tensions remained.

Unlike Elizabeth and Robert, for some older persons whose marriages may be in crisis, more direct and authority oriented methods of intervention may be in order. Counselors may need to say to those persons who are in the cohort of 1920 or earlier, such things as, "Stop saying that to your spouse!" "Say this instead." They are able to respond to the direct "advice" of the counselor, even when appeals to emotional support or cognitive considerations cannot be heard.[22] When the crisis subsides it may be possible to use less authority oriented methods, but it may not be with some couples who still are in need of help and who need specific direction.

   b. Family counseling. Although sometimes family counseling involving older people is indicated more because of the needs of children and grandchildren than those of the elderly as such, in other cases the needs of the elderly may be very much in view as well. Adapting to seeming reversal of parenting roles is a difficult thing for many—both elders and their children, for instance. In other instances children are made uncomfortable by their parents' seemingly inappropriate behavior—dating, going back to school, refusing to play the role of grandparent as they perceive it (baby-sitting their children). In yet another set of difficulties elderly parents attempt to keep children, even middle-aged children, from having to face full responsibility for their actions (particularly various forms of substance abuse) by financially subsidizing, emotionally encouraging dependency and thus manipulating them. The current word for this kind of family entanglement is codependency, which seems to me to be somewhat inadequate as a description of the dynamics of power needs and emotional seduction, mixed with genuine concern.

   As indicated earlier, I shall not sketch procedures for family counseling, since I believe it requires specialized training. I note that Florsheim and Herr have proposed a problem-solving model based in part on the work of Jay Haley, which they advocate for use with families who have an elderly member or members.[23] This model is designed to elicit cooperation through a direct inquiry about the problem in concrete terms, about what each person is doing to contain or resolve it, determining limited goals for treatment and carrying them out. It appears to me that this relatively direct, cooperative, model will be more effective than some others based on presumed underlying family dynamics.

   c. Group counseling. Counseling older persons in groups

is appropriate in some situations. Capuzzi, Gross, and Friel describe five types of groups for the elderly: reality-oriented groups in institutional settings, remotivation groups to provide stimulation in hospital or, possibly, day-care settings, reminiscing groups, which can work in church or senior center settings, psychotherapy groups which may be helpful with emotional issues, in hospital or day-care settings, and topic specific support groups, such as groups facilitating mourning or loss, but also for activities such as singing or poetry writing.[24] Although most pastoral caregivers would need additional training before leading such groups, they are often in a good position to facilitate the organization of groups in church settings, and sometimes in day-care settings. This is especially true of groups of widows and widowers, since ministers usually have had personal contact with them during the early stages of bereavement.

In concluding this chapter, I realize that much has been left unsaid about the procedures for the pastoral counseling of the elderly. But I believe that enough has been suggested to stimulate the reader, and that what has been said is sound. The reader might well ask, are there no special techniques for dealing with the possibility of encroaching disability, if not the actuality of it, and the nearing horizon of death? Although the counselor of the aging needs to be sensitive to these and other age-related issues, I think there are, indeed, no special techniques, except, perhaps, reminiscence. The elderly are just as human as others, and hence sound counseling procedures need only a little adapting, except that the awareness of infirmity and death coming make them a little more human. Always care needs to be taken to adapt the model to the person.

I shall offer no summary of this book, but rather a few remarks designed to highlight some key elements in it. In the earlier parts of the book a considerable effort was expended to try to dispel some of the effects of ageism as they affect pastoral caregivers of the elderly, since I am convinced that many of us have serious doubts about what might be called the *counselability* of the aging—doubts which prevent us from taking the possibilities seriously. I hope that this effort has been effective, and that the elderly are seen as fully human, compounded of self and spirit intertwined and embodied.

Pastoral counseling has been viewed as an important pastoral care ministry often neglected, but not as the only needed ministry to the aging. The social and cultural context is important as a factor in readiness for pastoral counseling among the elderly, with multilevel continuing care retirement communities of elderly seeming to provide the highest degree of readiness, followed by the age-integrated communities, and then finally by large, homeowner retirement communities.

Pastoral counseling will more often be appropriate for the "young old," but sometimes for those of very advanced years as well. It is especially appropriate for some of those suffering from the effects of grief reactions and the mild to moderate depression caused by these and other aspects of aging, anxieties related to identity, vocational, and spiritual uncertainty, as well as interpersonal and familial distress. Pastoral counseling can not only alleviate the suffering caused by these conditions, but when appropriate goals are formulated, often achieve positive changes in the sense cohesion and worth of self, and in the relational vectors of the spirit. New vistas of vocation, personal enrichment, and spiritual development can be opened.

Although pastoral counseling cannot provide all the resources needed for older persons to live as full and enriching lives as possible, it ministers to them at the crucial juncture of self and spirit as the most focal and specific of the pastoral care ministries. For their spirits, which have come from God and soon are to return to God, it can maximize their potential for giving to the world and receiving from it, even as the twilight deepens.

Notes

1. Anxieties and Dilemmas of the Elderly

1. Dorothy Dinnerstein, *The Mermaid and the Minotaur: Sexual Arrangements and Human Malaise* (San Francisco: Harper and Row, 1977), and Nancy Chodorow, *The Reproduction of Mothering: Psychoanalysis and the Sociology of Gender* (Berkeley: The University of California Press, 1978).

2. Don S. Browning, *Generative Man: Psychoanalytic Perspectives* (Philadelphia: Westminster Press, 1973), and Donald Capps, *Life Cycle Theory and Pastoral Care* (Philadelphia: Fortress Press, 1983).

3. William M. Clements, *Care and Counseling of the Aging* (Philadelphia: Fortress Press, 1979).

4. K. Byrnolf Lyon, *Toward a Practical Theology of Aging* (Philadelphia: Fortress Press, 1985).

5. Seward Hiltner, ed., *Toward a Theology of Aging* (New York: Human Sciences Press, 1975).

6. Carol LeFevre and Perry LeFevre, eds., *Aging and the Human Spirit* (Chicago: Exploration Press, 1981).

7. Eugene C. Bianchi, *Aging as a Spiritual Journey* (New York: Crossroad Press, 1989).

2. The Cultural Situation

1. Bennett S. Gurian and Marjorie H. Cantor, "Mental Health and Community Support Systems for the Elderly," in Gene Usdin and Charles K. Hofling, eds. (New York: Brunner/ Mazel, 1978), p. 197.

2. Robert N. Bellah, *Habits of the Heart: Individualism and*

Commitment in American Life (San Francisco: Harper and Row, 1986).

3. Gurian and Cantor, p. 195.

4. *Ibid.*, 195–196.

5. *Ibid.*

6. David R. Unruh, *Invisible Lives: Social Worlds of the Aged* (New York: Russell Sage Foundation, 1983), p. 14.

7. J. Gordon Harris, *Biblical Perspectives on Aging: God and the Elderly* (Philadelphia: Fortress Press, 1987), pp. 58–59.

8. *Ibid.*, pp. 77–84.

9. *Ibid.*, pp. 84–94.

10. *Ibid.*, p. 103.

11. *Hamlet*, Act I, Scene 3.

3. The Elderly as Human Beings

1. Robert Kegan, *The Evolving Self: Problem and Process in Human Development* (Cambridge: Harvard University Press, 1982).

2. K. Warner Schaie, "Quasi-experimental Research Designs in the Psychology of Aging," in James E. Birren and K. Warner Schaie, eds., *Handbook of the Psychology of Aging* (New York: van Nostrand Reinhold, 1977), p. 40.

3. Elaine Cumming and William E. Henry, *Growing Old: The Process of Disengagement* (New York: Basic Books, 1961).

4. Robert C. Atchley, "A Continuity Theory of Normal Aging," *The Gerontologist*, 29 (1989), 2, 183.

5. Takashi Makinodan, "Biology of Aging: Retrospect and Prospect," in Takashi Makinodan and Edmond Yunis, *Immunology and Aging* (New York: Plenum Press, 1977), pp. 1–8.

6. Fergus I. M. Craik, "Age Differences in Human Memory," in Birren and Schaie, *Handbook*, p. 386.

7. *Ibid.*, p. 387.

8. *Ibid.*, p. 394.

9. *Ibid.*, p. 399.

10. *Ibid.*, p. 400.

11. *Ibid.*, p. 409.

12. *The New York Times*, March 27, 1990.

13. Helen W. Lapsley, personal communication.

14. Suzanne Paterson Center, Princeton, New Jersey, 1989.

15. A. E. David Schonfield, "Learning, Memory, and Aging," in James E. Birren and R. Bruce Sloan, eds., *Handbook of Mental Health and Aging* (Englewood Cliffs, NJ: Prentice Hall, 1980), p. 218.

16. *Ibid.*

17. "Midlife: Aging Brain Loses Cells for Anxiety," *The New York Times*, April 21, 1987.

18. Alex Comfort, "Sexuality in Later Life," in Birren and Sloan, p. 886.

19. *Ibid.*, p. 887.

20. Nan Corby and Robert L. Solnick, "Psychosocial Influences on Sexuality in the Older Adult," in Birren and Sloan, pp. 896–897.

21. *Ibid.*, pp. 914–915.

22. R. W. Bartrop, *et al.*, "Depressed Lymphocyte Function after Bereavement," *Lancet*, 1977, 1:834–836.

23. Steven J. Schleifer, *et al.*, "Behavioral and Developmental Aspects of Immunity, *Journal of the American Academy of Child Psychiatry*, 26 (1986), 751–763.

24. W. Hijmans and C. F. Hollander, "The Pathogenic Role of Age-Related Immune Dysfunctions," in Makinodan and Yunis, p. 26.

25. Schleifer, pp. 751–752.

26. *Ibid.*, p. 752.

27. Hijmans and Hollander, pp. 28–30.

28. Schleifer, p. 754.

29. *Ibid.*, pp. 754–755.

30. R. Scott Sullender, *Losses in Later Life: A New Way of Walking with God* (Mahwah, NJ: Paulist Press, 1989), p. 4.

31. Raymond D. Adams, "The Morphological Aspects of Aging in the Human Nervous System," in Birren and Sloan, pp. 149–160.

32. Blossom T. Wignor, "Drives and Motivation with Aging," in Birren and Sloan, pp. 245–261.

33. *Ibid.*, 254.

34. James E. Birren and V. Jane Renner, "Concepts and Issues of Mental Health and Aging," in Birren and Sloan, pp. 22–23.

4. An Age Inclusive Model of Human Being: Spirit and Self

1. James N. Lapsley, "The 'Self,' Its Vicissitudes and Possibilities: An Essay in Theological Anthropology," *Pastoral Psychology*, 35, 1 (Fall, 1986), 23–45, and "Spirit and Self," *Pastoral Psychology*, 38, 3 (Spring, 1990), 135–146.

2. Wolfhart Pannenberg, "The Doctrine of the Spirit and the Task of a Theology of Nature," *Theology*, 75, 10.

3. Lapsley, 1986, 30.

4. H. Richard Niebuhr, *The Responsible Self: An Essay in Christian Moral Philosophy* (New York: Harper and Row, 1963), p. 85.

5. Pastoral Counseling as Pathway to the Future: An Overview of Its Purpose, Structure, and Processes

1. Charles V. Gerkin, "Pastoral Care and Models of Aging," *Journal of Religion and Aging*, 5/6, 1989, 83–100.

2. *Ibid.*, 95.

3. Louise O. Bernstein, "A Special Service: Counseling the Individual Elderly Client," *Generations*, XIV, 1 (Winter, 1990), 35–39.

4. *Ibid.*, 37.

5. *Ibid.*

6. Indicators for Pastoral Counseling: Needs and Situations

1. Colin Murray Parkes, *Bereavement: Studies of Grief in Adult Life* (New York: International Universities Press, 1972), p. 6.

2. Tori DeAngelis, "Study of Aging Paints Rosy Picture," *The APA Monitor*, 21, 8 (August, 1990), 11.

3. Walter S. Weinstein and Prabha Khanna, *Depression in the Elderly: Conceptual Issues and Psychotherapeutic Intervention* (New York: Philosophical Library, 1986), p. 23.

4. *Diagnostic and Statistical Manual of Mental Disorders*, Third Edition, Revised (Washington: American Psychiatric Association, 1987), p. 229.

5. Weinstein and Khanna, pp. 120–133.

6. *Ibid.*, pp. 69–103.

7. *Ibid.*, pp. 19, 89.

8. Hammer, M., "Psychotherapy with the Aged," in *The Theory and Practice of Psychotherapy with Specific Disorders* (Springfield, IL: Charles Thomas, 1972). Cited by Weinstein and Khanna, p. 95.

9. Pat M. Keith, "Life Changes and Perceptions of Life and Death Among Older Men and Women," in Carol LeFevre and Perry LeFevre, eds., *Aging and the Human Spirit* (Chicago: Exploration Press, 1981), pp. 197–205.

10. Phillip E. Hammond, "Aging and the Ministry," in LeFevre and LeFevre, p. 145.

11. Eugene C. Bianchi, *Aging As A Spiritual Journey* (New York: Crossroad, 1989), p. 225.

12. David Gutmann, *Reclaimed Powers: Toward a New Psychology of Men and Women in Later Life* (New York: Basic Books, 1987), pp. 4–5.

7. The Contexts of the Pastoral Counseling of the Elderly

1. Seward Hiltner and Lowell Colston, *The Context of Pastoral Counseling* (Nashville: Abingdon Press, 1961), pp. 29–31.

2. *Bulletin of the American Association of Retired Persons,* June, 1990.

3. "Strategies to Let Elderly Keep Some Control," *The New York Times*, March 28, 1990.

4. Tori DeAngelis, "Study on Aging Paints Rosy Picture," *APA Monitor*, 21, 8 (August, 1990), 11.

5. "Elderly Yuppies," *Eau Claire (Wis.) Leader*, July 15, 1990.

6. Frances Fitzgerald, *Cities on a Hill: A Journey Through Contemporary American Cultures* (Simon and Shuster, 1986), p. 212.

7. *Ibid.*, p. 232.

8. "Elderly Yuppies."

9. Gordon L. Bultena and Vivian Wood, "The American Retirement Community: Bane or Blessing?" *Journal of Gerontology*, 24 (1969), 209–217.

10. Frances Fitzgerald, p. 218. Data cited are from Sun City, FL., but seem applicable also to Sun City, AZ.

11. *Ibid.*, p. 244.

12. "A Desert Boomtown," *The Arizona Republic*, March 4, 1990.

13. Frances Fitzgerald, p. 205, *et passim.*

14. Bultena and Wood, 211–212.

15. *Ibid.*, 213–214.

16. Reed Larson, "Thirty Years of Research on the Subjective Well-Being of Older Americans," *Journal of Gerontology*, 33, 1 (1978), 109–125.

17. Neal E. Cutler, "Age Variations in the Dimensionality of Life Satisfaction," *Journal of Gerontology*, 34, 4 (1979), 573–578.

8. Goals of Pastoral Counseling with the Elderly

1. Arthur H. Becker, *Ministry with Older Persons: A Guide for Clergy and Congregations* (Minneapolis: Augsburg, 1986), p. 142.

2. Sharon R. Kaufman, *The Ageless Self: Sources of Meaning in Late Life* (Madison: University of Wisconsin Press, 1986), p. 25, *et passim.*

3. Margaret Clark and Barbara Anderson, *Culture and Aging* (Springfield, IL.: Charles Thomas, 1967. Cited in Kaufman, p. 6.

4. Kaufman, p. 64.

5. Peter G. Coleman, *Aging and Reminiscence Processes: Social and Clinical Implications* (John Wiley, 1986).

6. *Ibid.*, p. 37. 21 persons valued reminiscence, 8 were troubled by it, 15 saw no point in it, and 6 have to avoid it.

7. *Ibid.*, p. 35.

8. *Ibid.*, p. 27.

9. A. W. McMahon and P. J. Rhudick, "Reminiscing: Adaptational Significance in the Aged," *Archives of General Psychiatry*, 10: 292–298.

10. William A. Barry and William J. Connolly, *The Practice of Spiritual Direction* (New York: Seabury Press, 1982).

11. Robert J. Wicks, *Living Simply in an Anxious World* (Mahwah, NJ.: Paulist Press, 1988), and David J. Maitland, *Aging as a Counterculture: A Vocation for the Later Years* (New York: Pilgrim Press, 1991).

12. Richard S. Lazarus, "Cognition and Motivation in Emotion," *American Psychologist*, 46, 4 (April, 1991), 362.

13. Aaron T. Beck, *Cognitive Therapy and the Emotional Disorders*, (New York: International Universities Press, 1976), and Albert Ellis, *Reason and Emotion in Psychotherapy* (New York: Lyle Stuart, 1962).

14. "Cognitive-behavioral psychotherapy accepts these processes (e.g., belief systems, expectancies, attributions) as basic data and seeks also to fashion interventions and assess their effectiveness on the basis of sound scientific principles." Philip C. Kendall and Steven Hollon, eds., *Cognitive-Behavioral Interventions: Theory, Research, and Procedures* (New York: Academic Press, 1979), p. xv.

15. Michael A. Smyer and Robert Inrieri, "Evaluating Counseling Outcomes," *Generations*, XIV, 4 (Winter, 1990), 11–14.

16. Arthur Freeman, "Cognitive Therapy: An Overview," in Arthur Freeman and Vincent Greenwood, *Cognitive Therapy: Applications in Psychiatric and Medical Settings* (New York: Human Sciences Press, 1987), p. 19.

17. Aaron T. Beck, "Cognitive Therapy: A 30 Year Retrospective," *American Psychologist*, 46, 4 (April, 1991), 368–375.

18. Arthur Freeman, pp. 21–22.

19. *Ibid.*, p. 22.

20. Meyer D. Glanz, "Cognitive Therapy with the Elderly," in Arthur Freeman, *et al.*, eds. *Comprehensive Handbook of Cognitive Therapy* (New York: Plenum Press, 1989), pp. 467–490.

9. Procedures for Pastoral Counseling with The Elderly

1. Meyer D. Glanz, "Cognitive Therapy with the Elderly," Arthur Freeman, *et al.*, eds., *Comprehensive Handbook of Cognitive Therapy* (New York: Plenum Press, 1989, p. 484.

2. Seward Hiltner, *Pastoral Counseling* (New York: Abingdon-Cokesbury, 1949), and Carroll A. Wise, *Pastoral Counseling: Its Theory and Practice* (New York: Harper, 1951). Both Hiltner and Wise claimed a degree of independence from Rogers, and some hospital chaplains in the clinical pastoral education movement practiced empathy and taught it to their students in the 1940s.

3. Howard W. Stone, "Depression," in Howard W. Stone and William M. Clements, eds., *Handbook for Basic Types of Pastoral Counseling* (Nashville: Abingdon, 1990), p. 206.

4. "Reattribution" is one among the several procedural categories drawn from a list discussed by Arthur Freeman, "Cognitive Therapy: An Overview," in Arthur Freeman and Vincent Greenwood, eds., *Cognitive Therapy: Applications in Psychiatric and Medical Settings* (New York: Human Sciences Press, 1987), pp. 29–33. Others are: questioning the evidence, decatastrophizing, fantasized consequences, advantages and disadvantages, turning adversity to advantage, labeling of distortions, paradox or exaggeration—humor, scaling, examining options and alternatives, cognitive rehearsal, replacement imagery, active scheduling, mastery and pleasure ratings, behavioral rehearsal, bibliotherapy, relaxation, and *in vivo work.*

5. Aaron T. Beck, *et al., Cognitive Therapy of Depression* (New York: Guilford Press, 1979), p. 159.

6. *Ibid.*, p. 72.

7. *Ibid.*

8. Arthur Freeman, p. 31.

9. Christie Cozad Neuger, "Imagination in Pastoral Care and Counseling," in Stone and Clements, p. 160.

10. *Ibid.*

11. David J. A. Edwards, "Cognitive Restructuring through Guided Imagery: Lessons from Gestalt Therapy," in Freeman, *et al., Comprehensive Handbook,* p. 284.

12. Stone, p. 204.

13. Howard W. Stone, *Using Behavioral Methods in Pastoral Counseling* (Philadelphia: Fortress Press, 1981), pp. 60–80.

14. Beck, *et al.*, p. 273.

15. Norman Epstein and Donald H. Baucom, "Cognitive-

Behavioral Marital Therapy," in Freeman, *et al.*, *Comprehensive Handbook*, p. 492.

16. *Ibid.*, p. 493.

17. *Ibid.*

18. *Ibid.*, p. 494.

19. *Ibid.*

20. *Ibid.*, p. 496.

21. *Ibid.*, p. 497.

22. Duane Halloran, Interfaith Counseling Service, Phoenix, AZ, personal communication.

23. Margaret Florsheim and John J. Herr, "Family Counseling with Elders," *Generations*, XIV, 1 (Winter, 1990), 40–42.

24. Dave Capuzzi, Doug Gross, and Susan Eileen Friel, "Recent Trends in Group Work with Elders," *Generations*, XIV, 1 (Winter, 1990), 143–148.